W9-BYF-347

# Eyewitness
# BUTTERFLY
# & MOTH

Pyralid moth,
*Margaronia
quadrimaculata*
(China)

Smaller Wood Nymph butterfly,
*Ideopsis gaura*
(Indonesia)

White Satin
moth caterpillar,
*Leucoma salicis*
(Europe and Asia)

Noctuid moth,
*Diphthera
hieroglyphica*
(Central
America)

Madagascan Moon moth,
*Argema mittrei*
(Madagascar)

Eyed Hawk-moth
caterpillar,
*Smerinthus ocellata*
(Europe and Asia)

Thyridid moth,
*Rhondoneura limatula*
(Madagascar)

Red Glider butterfly,
*Cymothoe coccinata*
(Africa)

Lasiocampid moth,
*Gloveria gargemella*
(North America)

Tailed Jay butterfly,
*Graphium agamemnon*
(Asia and Australia)

Jersey Tiger moth,
*Euplagia
quadripunctaria*
(Europe and Asia)

Arctiid moth,
*Composia credula*
(North and South America)

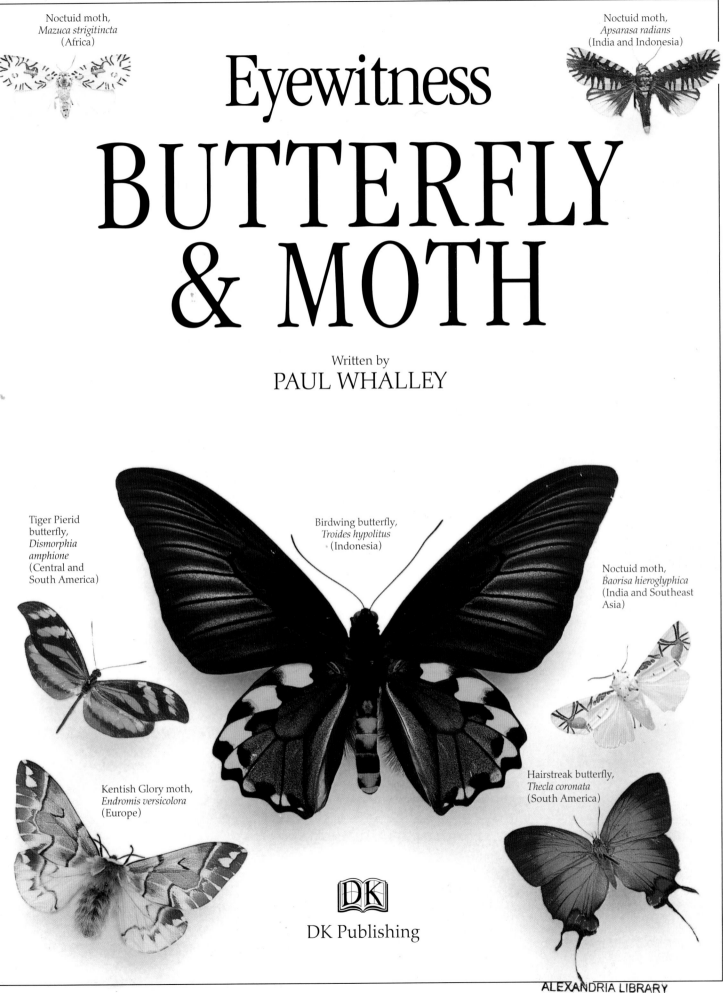

Noctuid moth,
*Mazuca strigitincta*
(Africa)

Noctuid moth,
*Apsarasa radians*
(India and Indonesia)

# Eyewitness
# BUTTERFLY
# & MOTH

Written by
PAUL WHALLEY

Tiger Pierid
butterfly,
*Dismorphia
amphione*
(Central and
South America)

Birdwing butterfly,
*Troides hypolitus*
(Indonesia)

Noctuid moth,
*Baorisa hieroglyphica*
(India and Southeast
Asia)

Kentish Glory moth,
*Endromis versicolora*
(Europe)

Hairstreak butterfly,
*Thecla coronata*
(South America)

## DK Publishing

ALEXANDRIA LIBRARY
ALEXANDRIA, VA 22304

Peacock butterfly,
*Inachis io*
(Europe and Asia)

Geometrid moth, *Rhodophitus simplex*
(South Africa)

Roseate Emperor moth, *Euchroa trimeni*
(South Africa)

Pyralid moth,
*Ethopia roseilinea*
(Southeast Asia)

Lappet moth,
*Gastropacha quercifolia*
(Europe and Asia)

# DK

## LONDON, NEW YORK,
## MELBOURNE, MUNICH, and DELHI

**Project editor** Michele Byam
**Managing art editor** Jane Owen
**Special photography** Colin Keates
(Natural History Museum, London),
Kim Taylor, and Dave King

REVISED EDITION
**Revised by** David Burnie

DK INDIA
**Project editor** Nidhi Sharma
**Project art editor** Rajnish Kashyap
**Editor** Pallavi Singh
**Designer** Honlung Zach Ragui
**Managing editor** Saloni Talwar
**Managing art editor** Romi Chakraborty
**DTP designer** Tarun Sharma
**Picture researcher** Sumedha Chopra

DK UK
**Senior editor** Dr. Rob Houston
**Senior art editor** Philip Letsu
**Production editor** Adam Stoneham
**Production controller** Rebecca Short
**Publisher** Andrew Macintyre

DK US
**US editor** Margaret Parrish
**Editorial director** Nancy Ellwood

This revised edition published in the United States in 2012
by DK Publishing, 375 Hudson Street,
New York, New York 10014
First published in the United States in 2000

10 9 8 7 6 5 4 3 2 1

001—183527—July/12

Copyright © 2000, © 2012 Dorling Kindersley Limited
All rights reserved under International and Pan-American Copyright
Conventions. No part of this publication may be reproduced, stored in a
retrieval system, or transmitted in any form or by any means, electronic,
mechanical, photocopying, recording, or otherwise, without the prior written
permission of the copyright owner. Published in Great Britain
by Dorling Kindersley Limited.

DK books are available at special discounts when purchased in bulk for sales
promotions, premiums, fundraising, or educational use. For details, contact: DK
Publishing Special Markets 375 Hudson Street, New York, New York 10014
SpecialSales@dk.com

A catalog record for this book is available from the Library of Congress.

ISBN: 978-0-7566-9298-8 (Hardcover)
ISBN: 978-0-7566-9299-5 (ALB)

Color reproduction by Colourscan, Singapore
Printed and bound in China
by Toppan Printing Co. (Shenzhen) Ltd.

Discover more at
## www.dk.com

Swallowtail butterfly,
*Papilio machaon*
(North America,
Europe, and Asia)

White Satin moth
caterpillar,
*Leucoma salicis*
(Europe and Asia)

Privet
Hawkmoth
caterpillar, *Sphinx
ligustri* (Europe
and Asia)

African Migrant butterfly,
*Catopsilia florella* (Africa)

Cloudless Giant
Sulfur butterfly,
*Phoebis sennae*
(North and
Central America)

# Contents

Giant Purple
Emperor (Japanese
national butterfly),
*Sasakia charonda*
(Southeast Asia)

# Butterfly or moth?

Butterflies and moths are the most popular and easily recognizable of insects. Together, the two groups make up a large group (or order) of insects known as the Lepidoptera (from the Greek words for "scale" and "wing"). The order is divided into families of butterflies and moths, containing about 170,000 known species. The division of Lepidoptera into butterflies and moths is an artificial one, based on a number of observable differences. For example, most butterflies fly by day and most moths fly by night; many butterflies are brightly colored and many moths are dull-colored; most butterflies hold their wings upright over their backs, while most moths rest with their wings flat; butterfly antennae are knobbed at the tip, but moth antennae are either featherlike or plain. However, despite these rules, there is not one single feature that separates all butterflies from all moths.

**MEDIEVAL BUTTERFLY**
A beautifully painted Red Admiral decorates a 16th-century Flemish manuscript, *Hours of Anne of Brittany*.

*Wings folded over back*

*Antenna without club*

*Fat abdomen*

**SPOT THE DIFFERENCE**
There are several ways to tell which of these two insects is a hawkmoth from Africa, *Euchloron megaera*, and which is a Blue Morpho butterfly, *Morpho peleides*, from Central America. Like many moths, the hawkmoth has a fat abdomen. It also has a moth's typical simple or feathery antennae, rather than the butterfly's club-tipped antennae. And if you had a magnifying glass, you could see that only the moth has a tiny hook and bristle linking its forewings and hind wings.

# A short life, but a long history

It seems strange to think of graceful moths flying around giant dinosaurs, but from fossils we can tell that the first primitive moths lived about 140 million years ago. Butterflies evolved later than moths, the oldest fossils discovered so far being about 40 million years old. By the time the first people appeared, about 5 million years ago, butterflies and moths were like those we see today.

**AMERICAN PIONEER** *left*
This 40-million-year old specimen of a Nymphalid butterfly, *Prodryas persephone*, was found in the fossil beds of Lake Florissant, Colorado, USA.

**EGYPTIAN TOMB PAINTING**
The ancient Egyptians believed that in the afterworld the dead could still hunt birds and see butterflies by the banks of the Nile River.

# Lepidoptera versus the rest

After looking at the differences between butterflies and moths, it is interesting to see how they differ structurally from other orders of insect. All insects have three main divisions to their bodies—head, thorax, and abdomen. Insects have their "skeleton" around the body, not inside like mammals. If an insect's body were an undivided "tube", it would have great difficulty moving—dividing the tube up into segments gives greater flexibility. Structurally, butterflies and moths are like all other insects, but their most obvious difference is the scale covering on wings and body. Their ability to coil up the feeding tube, or proboscis is also unique. All insects have six legs attached to the thorax, although some butterflies have shorter front legs. Insects are the only invertebrates with wings, although not all insects, including some female moths, can fly.

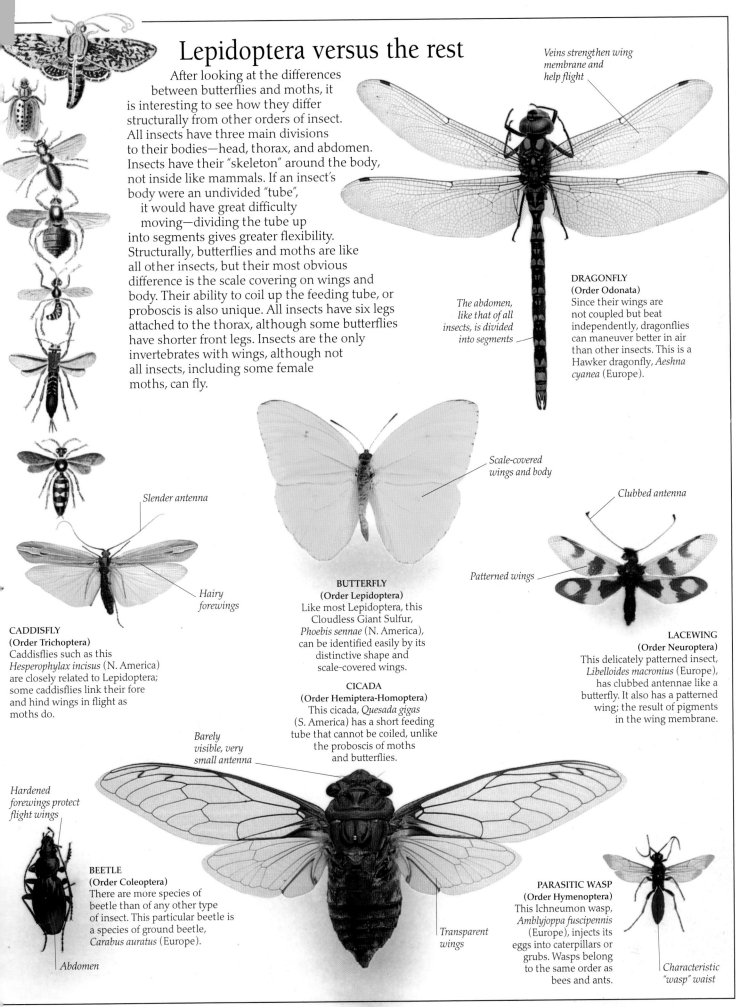

*Veins strengthen wing membrane and help flight*

*The abdomen, like that of all insects, is divided into segments*

**DRAGONFLY**
**(Order Odonata)**
Since their wings are not coupled but beat independently, dragonflies can maneuver better in air than other insects. This is a Hawker dragonfly, *Aeshna cyanea* (Europe).

*Scale-covered wings and body*

*Clubbed antenna*

*Patterned wings*

*Slender antenna*

*Hairy forewings*

**CADDISFLY**
**(Order Trichoptera)**
Caddisflies such as this *Hesperophylax incisus* (N. America) are closely related to Lepidoptera; some caddisflies link their fore and hind wings in flight as moths do.

**BUTTERFLY**
**(Order Lepidoptera)**
Like most Lepidoptera, this Cloudless Giant Sulfur, *Phoebis sennae* (N. America), can be identified easily by its distinctive shape and scale-covered wings.

**CICADA**
**(Order Hemiptera-Homoptera)**
This cicada, *Quesada gigas* (S. America) has a short feeding tube that cannot be coiled, unlike the proboscis of moths and butterflies.

**LACEWING**
**(Order Neuroptera)**
This delicately patterned insect, *Libelloides macronius* (Europe), has clubbed antennae like a butterfly. It also has a patterned wing; the result of pigments in the wing membrane.

*Barely visible, very small antenna*

*Hardened forewings protect flight wings*

**BEETLE**
**(Order Coleoptera)**
There are more species of beetle than of any other type of insect. This particular beetle is a species of ground beetle, *Carabus auratus* (Europe).

*Abdomen*

*Transparent wings*

**PARASITIC WASP**
**(Order Hymenoptera)**
This Ichneumon wasp, *Amblyjoppa fuscipennis* (Europe), injects its eggs into caterpillars or grubs. Wasps belong to the same order as bees and ants.

*Characteristic "wasp" waist*

# The life of a butterfly

THE LIFE CYCLE OF A BUTTERFLY OR MOTH consists of four different stages: egg, caterpillar, pupa, and adult. The length of the life cycle, from egg to adult, varies enormously between species. It may be as little as a few weeks if the insect lives in the high temperatures of buildings such as grain silos, like some of the Pyralid moths. Other moths may live for several years. Sometimes most of the cycle takes place concealed from human view. For example, most of the life cycle of the leaf-mining moth takes place between the upper and lower surfaces of a single leaf, with only the adult emerging into the outside world. In a similar way, some of the wood-boring larvae of the Cossid moths may spend months, or even years, in the caterpillar stage, hidden inside a tree. Other species pass their entire life cycle much more exposed. These are usually either well camouflaged or distasteful to predators. There are many variations on the life cycle—some species, for example, having fewer molts in the caterpillar stage than others. These two pages illustrate the life cycle of a South American Owl butterfly, *Caligo beltrao* (also pp. 16, 23, 35).

*Young caterpillar with new, green skin*

*Older caterpillar with brown skin is about to pupate*

## 1 EGGS
The eggs of the Owl butterfly have delicate ribs that meet at the top. The ribbing and the structure of the shell (a tough coating like an insect's body, not a brittle one like a hen's egg) are designed to protect the egg from water loss while allowing it to "breathe" (pp. 12–13).

## 2 CATERPILLARS
Once the caterpillar hatches, it feeds and grows rapidly. It molts its restrictive skin, developing a new one underneath, which stretches and allows new growth after the molt. Some species of *Caligo* are pests on bananas in Central and South America. The long, slender shape of the caterpillar helps to conceal it against the midrib of the leaves on which it feeds (p. 16).

**MEAT-EATING MOTH** *left*
The Pyralid *Laetilia coccicidivora* (N. and S. America) has a similar life cycle to other moths (pp. 36–37). It differs in the feeding habits of the caterpillar, which is predatory and eats scale insects and greenfly that it catches as it moves across the plant.

**SILK SPINNER** *right*
The life cycle of the Wild Silk moth, *Samia cynthia* (India), shows all the typical stages, but since it is a moth, it spins a cocoon in which to pupate (pp. 38–39). The caterpillar of this moth feeds on a variety of plants, including the Castor-oil plant, *Ricinus* (right). It also spins a dense cocoon.

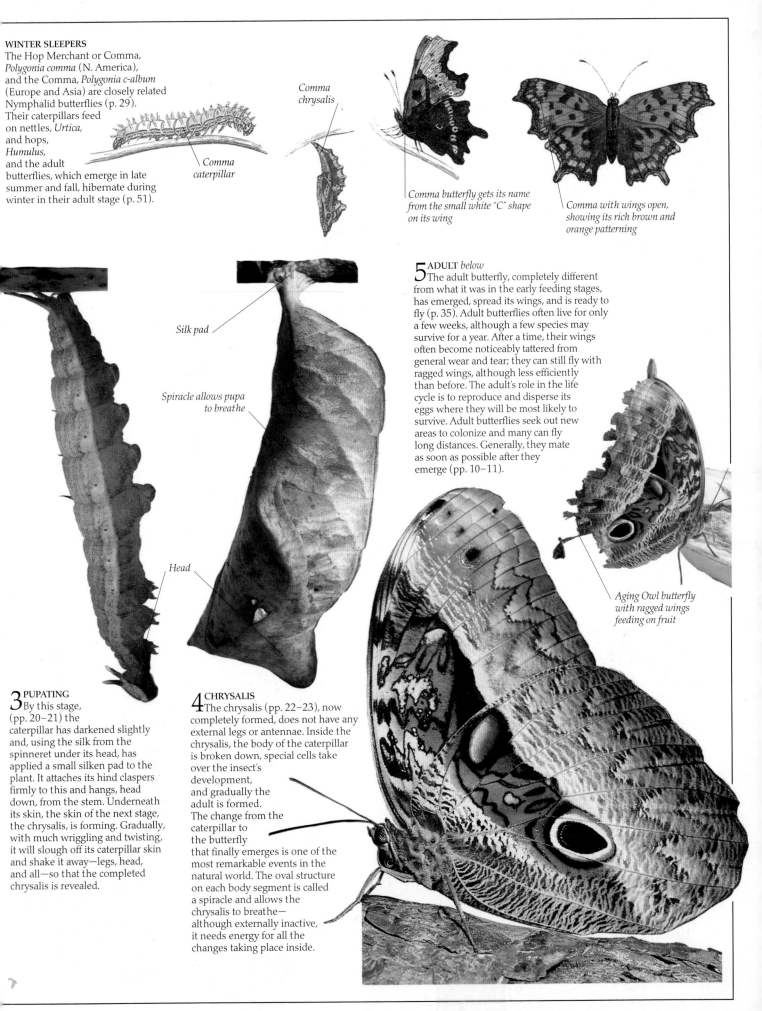

## WINTER SLEEPERS

The Hop Merchant or Comma, *Polygonia comma* (N. America), and the Comma, *Polygonia c-album* (Europe and Asia) are closely related Nymphalid butterflies (p. 29). Their caterpillars feed on nettles, *Urtica*, and hops, *Humulus*, and the adult butterflies, which emerge in late summer and fall, hibernate during winter in their adult stage (p. 51).

*Comma caterpillar*

*Comma chrysalis*

*Comma butterfly gets its name from the small white "C" shape on its wing*

*Comma with wings open, showing its rich brown and orange patterning*

**5 ADULT** *below*
The adult butterfly, completely different from what it was in the early feeding stages, has emerged, spread its wings, and is ready to fly (p. 35). Adult butterflies often live for only a few weeks, although a few species may survive for a year. After a time, their wings often become noticeably tattered from general wear and tear; they can still fly with ragged wings, although less efficiently than before. The adult's role in the life cycle is to reproduce and disperse its eggs where they will be most likely to survive. Adult butterflies seek out new areas to colonize and many can fly long distances. Generally, they mate as soon as possible after they emerge (pp. 10–11).

*Silk pad*

*Spiracle allows pupa to breathe*

*Head*

*Aging Owl butterfly with ragged wings feeding on fruit*

**3 PUPATING**
By this stage, (pp. 20–21) the caterpillar has darkened slightly and, using the silk from the spinneret under its head, has applied a small silken pad to the plant. It attaches its hind claspers firmly to this and hangs, head down, from the stem. Underneath its skin, the skin of the next stage, the chrysalis, is forming. Gradually, with much wriggling and twisting, it will slough off its caterpillar skin and shake it away—legs, head, and all—so that the completed chrysalis is revealed.

**4 CHRYSALIS**
The chrysalis (pp. 22–23), now completely formed, does not have any external legs or antennae. Inside the chrysalis, the body of the caterpillar is broken down, special cells take over the insect's development, and gradually the adult is formed. The change from the caterpillar to the butterfly that finally emerges is one of the most remarkable events in the natural world. The oval structure on each body segment is called a spiracle and allows the chrysalis to breathe—although externally inactive, it needs energy for all the changes taking place inside.

# Courtship and egg-laying

THE MOST IMPORTANT EVENTS in the lives of butterflies and moths are mating and the laying of eggs. The striking colors and shapes of many species are thought to attract the opposite sex. In addition, most butterflies and moths have complicated courtship behavior. In addition to performing elaborate courtship flights and "dances," they often use chemicals called pheromones to attract members of the opposite sex. "Assembling"—the attraction of males to females by scent—is now known to be due to these chemicals. In butterflies, it is usually the male who produces these powerful scents, while in moths it is often the female. When a male finds a female who shows an interest in him, they both land. The female holds her wings in a partly open position so that the male can land easily alongside her and continue spreading his scent. The mating pair will often tap one another with their antennae, detecting other scents that stimulate activity at close range. Mating may last for about 20 minutes, or for several hours, during which time the two insects do not move.

A 19th-century version of the butterflies' courtship dance

*Female Lackey moth*

**FROM EGG TO CATERPILLAR**
This moth, *Malacosoma neustria* (Europe), has a hairy caterpillar that eats the leaves of many trees. The moth's eggs are shown on the opposite page.

*Male Sweet Oil butterfly*

*Female Sweet Oil butterfly*

**BUTTERFLIES MATING**
Like this pair of Sweet Oil butterflies, *Mechanitis polymnia* (S. America), most butterflies mate on a plant. They can fly while linked together, but they do not do this unless disturbed, so as not to call attention to themselves. After mating, males look for another female, but the mated females look for a particular plant to lay their eggs on. Some butterflies, notably those with grass-feeding larvae, scatter their eggs, but most females actively look for a food plant for the caterpillars.

## A TWO-HEADED BUTTERFLY?

A mating pair, like these two Asian swallowtails, can look like a two-headed butterfly. The tail-to-tail position links the genitalia of male and female together. The male has a complicated series of structures, including claspers, which he uses to grasp the female's abdomen. The genital organs of butterflies and moths are a useful way of identifying species.

*Female swallowtail*

*Male swallowtail*

## SEXUAL DIFFERENCES *right and below right*

The males and females of some butterfly species are widely different in external appearance, a condition known as sexual dimorphism. An example is the Orange tip, *Anthocharis cardamines* (Europe and Asia), in which the males have a distinctive orange color on the wingtips, while the females have black wingtips. In some species, the females are larger than the males, while a few female moths are flightless (p. 30).

*Male Orange tip has brightly colored orange wingtips*

*Female Orange tip has black wingtips*

# Egg-laying

After selecting the correct plant for the caterpillars, the female walks over a leaf, testing it carefully, presumably to make sure it belongs to the right plant species. We know that many species can detect chemicals from different plants: cabbage-eating Large and Small White butterflies, *Pieris brassicae* (Europe) and *Pieris rapae* (Europe, N. America, and Australia), have been persuaded to lay eggs on plants that their caterpillars will not eat, by putting traces of extract from cabbages on the surface of the leaves.

## SILK MOTH LAYING EGGS *left*

This female silk moth has laid her batch of eggs on a mulberry leaf. Although this moth may lay many eggs in the wild, few of them will become adults. But in artificial conditions, large numbers of moths can be raised from one egg batch (see pp. 40–41).

*Egg*

## DELICATE OPERATION

This Pierid butterfly from Central America, *Perrhybris pyra*, is laying its eggs on the upper surface of the leaf. She is very vulnerable to disturbance here, and a heavy rainstorm will interrupt egg-laying.

## SITES FOR EGG-LAYING

Some species of *Heliconius* butterfly lay their eggs on tendrils of the passion flower (above). The Lackey moth (see opposite page) lays its eggs in a ring around a twig, so that they look like part of the plant (below).

*Eggs*

## ABOUT TO HATCH *right*

These eggs of the Blue Mormon butterfly, *Papilio polymnestor* (Asia), have darkened and are about to hatch. Soon, tiny caterpillars will emerge (p. 18). A Blue Mormon lays its eggs in a random pattern rather than a cluster, so there is more chance that predatory bugs will overlook some of them.

*Egg under leaf*

# An emerging caterpillar

BUTTERFLIES AND MOTHS usually lay large numbers of eggs. The number varies greatly; some females lay over 1,000, although only a few eggs may survive to become adults. Eggs vary greatly from one species to another in their color and in their surface texture, which can be smooth or beautifully sculptured. The two main types are a flattened oval shape, usually with a smooth surface, and a more upright shape, which often has a heavily ribbed surface. In most cases, the female lays the eggs on a leaf or stem (see pp. 10–11), but some species—particularly the grass-feeding butterflies—simply release their eggs in flight. Both methods are designed to place the caterpillar as near as possible to the plant on which it feeds. These two pages show a caterpillar of a South American Owl butterfly (see pp. 8–9, 16, 23, and 25) hatching from its egg.

*Pattern of ridges can be a useful aid to identification of eggs*

*Actual size of egg*

*Darker color shows that egg will soon be ready to hatch*

**THE EGGS IN POSITION**
The Owl butterfly lays its eggs in groups. The color of the individual eggs can vary in this species. They turn darker as the time of hatching gets near.

**RESTING**
In many temperate butterflies and moths, fall-laid eggs usually go into a resting stage called "diapause" to pass the winter. This state is broken by low or fluctuating temperatures.

**WARMING UP**
Once winter diapause has broken and the temperature has risen enough for the caterpillar to stand a chance of survival, the egg darkens in color as the tiny caterpillar gets ready to emerge.

**EMERGING HEADFIRST**
The caterpillar seems to have a disproportionately large head and jaws, but the enormous mouthparts are useful for biting an opening in the eggshell. Nevertheless, it can be quite difficult for the small caterpillar to extract itself from the egg headfirst. The dark spots on each side of the head are simple eyes called ocelli. The caterpillar also gets information about its surroundings from its tiny antennae.

**CUTTING A CIRCLE**
In order to hatch, the caterpillar must bite its way through the shell of the egg. This is not a hard, brittle shell like that of a hen's egg, but it still poses a tough task for the minute caterpillar. Its jaws have to cut a circle big enough for the head to come out.

*Head of caterpillar starting to appear*

*Opening where caterpillar's jaws have cut through egg shell*

*Ocelli*

*Antenna*

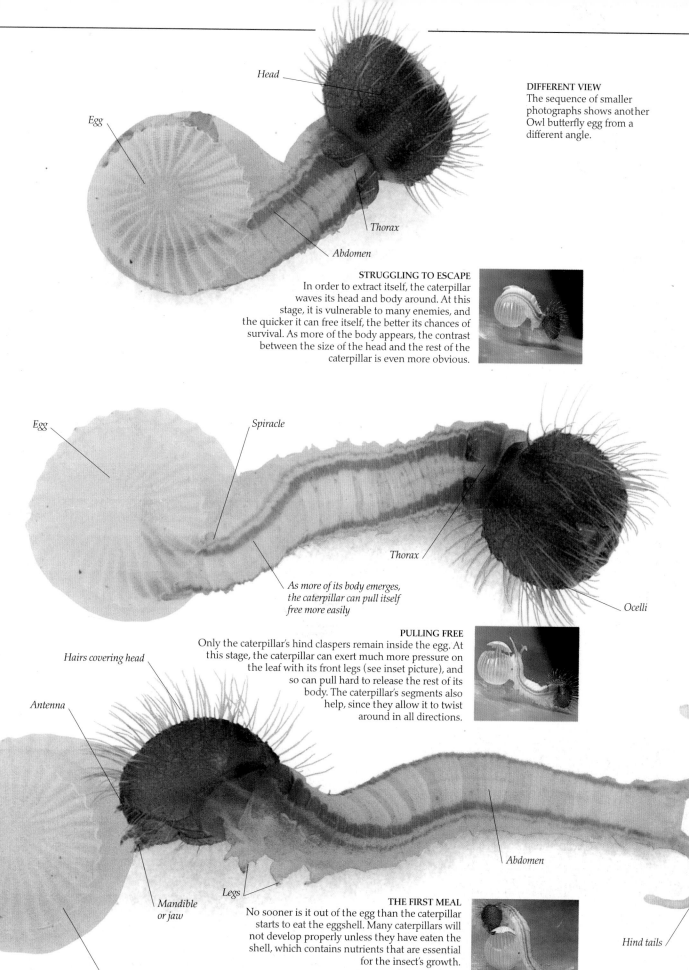

Head

Egg

DIFFERENT VIEW
The sequence of smaller photographs shows another Owl butterfly egg from a different angle.

Thorax

Abdomen

**STRUGGLING TO ESCAPE**
In order to extract itself, the caterpillar waves its head and body around. At this stage, it is vulnerable to many enemies, and the quicker it can free itself, the better its chances of survival. As more of the body appears, the contrast between the size of the head and the rest of the caterpillar is even more obvious.

Egg

Spiracle

*As more of its body emerges, the caterpillar can pull itself free more easily*

Thorax

Ocelli

**PULLING FREE**
Only the caterpillar's hind claspers remain inside the egg. At this stage, the caterpillar can exert much more pressure on the leaf with its front legs (see inset picture), and so can pull hard to release the rest of its body. The caterpillar's segments also help, since they allow it to twist around in all directions.

Hairs covering head

Antenna

Abdomen

Mandible or jaw

Legs

**THE FIRST MEAL**
No sooner is it out of the egg than the caterpillar starts to eat the eggshell. Many caterpillars will not develop properly unless they have eaten the shell, which contains nutrients that are essential for the insect's growth.

Hind tails

*Ribbed surface enables empty egg to keep its shape*

# Caterpillars

I**T IS A PITY THAT THE CATERPILLAR** is usually dismissed simply as a "feeding tube" because it is a complex and interesting stage in the life cycle of a butterfly or moth. Caterpillars carry in their bodies the cells that eventually produce an adult insect. They molt several times during their lives, discarding their outer skin to reveal a new, more elastic skin in which they can grow. Caterpillars are usually very active during this stage and need food and oxygen to grow and sustain themselves. However, they do not have lungs like mammals. They take in air through small holes called spiracles in the sides of their bodies. The air passes along fine tubes, or tracheoles, from which the oxygen is extracted by the body fluid. Caterpillars have a nervous system with a primitive "brain," or cerebral ganglion, in the head. The head itself is equipped with sense organs to tell the caterpillar what is going on in the world around it. These include short antennae and often a half circle of simple, light-sensitive "eyes," or ocelli. Also on the head are the massive jaws needed for chewing plant food. An essential feature of caterpillars, not present in the adult, is their ability to produce silk from special glands, and to force it out through a spinneret under the head (pp. 40–41).

The Caterpillar talking to Alice from *Alice in Wonderland* by Lewis Carroll

*Spine or horn at tip of abdomen*

*Abdomen*

*Four pairs of prolegs*

*Anal clasper*

**CATERPILLAR OF DEATH'S-HEAD HAWKMOTH (adult moth below)**

**BEDSTRAW HAWKMOTH** *right*
The caterpillar of the Bedstraw Hawkmoth, *Celerio galii*, feeds, as its name implies, on the bedstraw plant, *Galium.* The moth is found all over Europe and Asia, although it does not overwinter in the more northerly parts. Similar North American species include the tomato pest known as the Tobacco Hornworm *or* Carolina Sphinx, *Manduca sexta.*

**ADULT**
The Death's-head Hawkmoth, *Acherontia atropos* (Europe, Asia, and Africa), gets its name from the skull-like marking on its thorax. The adult moth (also p. 43) has the ability to squeak if handled, whereas the caterpillar only makes a clicking sound.

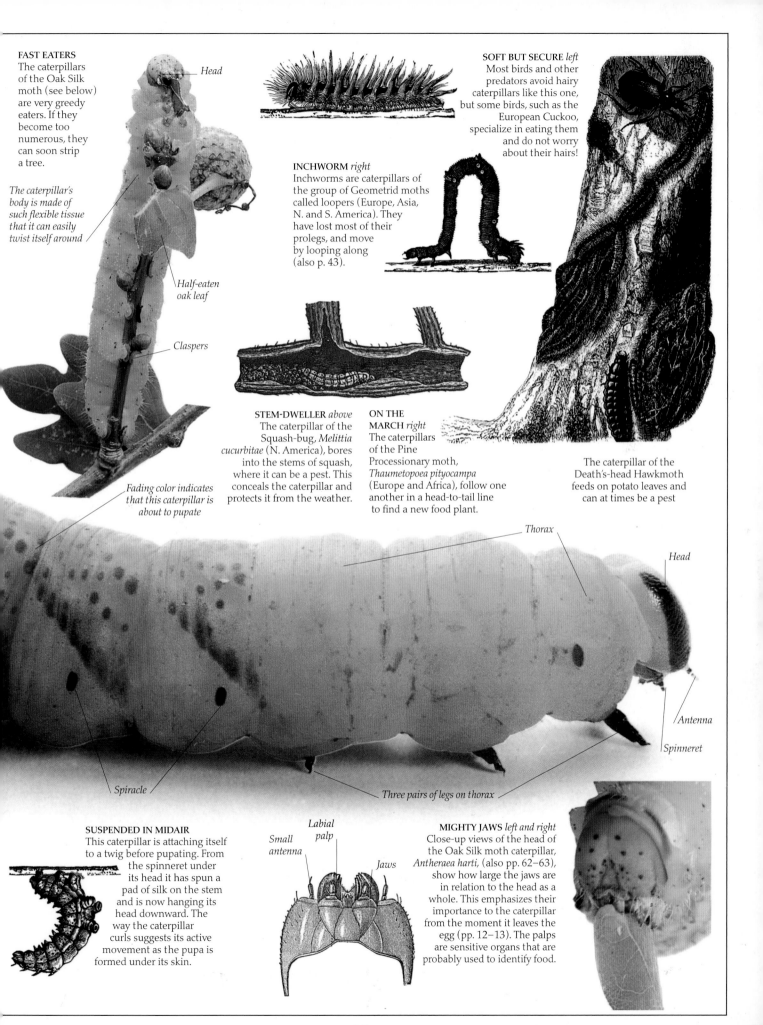

**FAST EATERS**
The caterpillars of the Oak Silk moth (see below) are very greedy eaters. If they become too numerous, they can soon strip a tree.

*The caterpillar's body is made of such flexible tissue that it can easily twist itself around*

Head

*Half-eaten oak leaf*

*Claspers*

*Fading color indicates that this caterpillar is about to pupate*

**SOFT BUT SECURE** *left*
Most birds and other predators avoid hairy caterpillars like this one, but some birds, such as the European Cuckoo, specialize in eating them and do not worry about their hairs!

**INCHWORM** *right*
Inchworms are caterpillars of the group of Geometrid moths called loopers (Europe, Asia, N. and S. America). They have lost most of their prolegs, and move by looping along (also p. 43).

**STEM-DWELLER** *above*
The caterpillar of the Squash-bug, *Melittia cucurbitae* (N. America), bores into the stems of squash, where it can be a pest. This conceals the caterpillar and protects it from the weather.

**ON THE MARCH** *right*
The caterpillars of the Pine Processionary moth, *Thaumetopoea pityocampa* (Europe and Africa), follow one another in a head-to-tail line to find a new food plant.

The caterpillar of the Death's-head Hawkmoth feeds on potato leaves and can at times be a pest

Thorax

Head

Antenna

Spinneret

*Three pairs of legs on thorax*

*Spiracle*

**SUSPENDED IN MIDAIR**
This caterpillar is attaching itself to a twig before pupating. From the spinneret under its head it has spun a pad of silk on the stem and is now hanging its head downward. The way the caterpillar curls suggests its active movement as the pupa is formed under its skin.

Small antenna

Labial palp

Jaws

**MIGHTY JAWS** *left and right*
Close-up views of the head of the Oak Silk moth caterpillar, *Antheraea harti*, (also pp. 62–63), show how large the jaws are in relation to the head as a whole. This emphasizes their importance to the caterpillar from the moment it leaves the egg (pp. 12–13). The palps are sensitive organs that are probably used to identify food.

# Exotic caterpillars

**FUZZY BEARS** *left and below*
The long hairs of many Arctiid moths"—fuzzy bears"—can cause allergic reactions in some people.

Aside from being efficient at feeding and growing, caterpillars must be able to survive in a hostile world. While caterpillars are an essential food source for birds to feed their young, it is clearly a disadvantage to be on the daily menu. This is why caterpillars have adopted a large variety of shapes and protective devices in order to survive. The caterpillars shown on the next four pages all come from tropical countries (see pp. 32–35 and 44–47) where, as in all wild places, "eat or be eaten" is very much the rule. Birds, mammals, and even certain predatory insects relish a juicy caterpillar. Fortunately for the caterpillars, many tropical species feed on plants whose contents may be poisonous. By absorbing the poisons and advertising their distastefulness with their bright colors, great numbers of caterpillars avoid an early death.

Owl butterfly, *Caligo beltrao*, (S. and C. America)

Flambeau, *Dryas iulia*, (N., C., and S. America)

These caterpillars are not fully grown (Owl caterpillars also on p. 8)

**TINY TIGER**
Like its relative, the Monarch, the brightly colored caterpillar of the Plain Tiger likes to advertise its presence. It is possible that the filaments sticking out of the caterpillar's body give it further protection by giving off an unpleasant smell.

Plain Tiger, *Danaus chrysippus*, (Africa, S. E. Asia, and Australia)

**GROUP OF OWLS**
The coloring of these Owl butterfly caterpillars (also pp. 8–9) makes them less conspicuous along the rib of the plant. The caterpillars have a series of filaments at their heads and tails that probably help to break up their outline.

Bright stripes act as a warning to its enemies

Species of passionflower (Passiflora)

Monarch, *Danaus plexippus* (Australia, N. and S. America)

Filaments

Zebra, *Heliconius charitonius* (N., C., and S. America)

**WARNINGLY COLORED**
Monarch caterpillars can retain poisonous substances from their milkweed and dogbane food plants. Once a bird has pecked one of these caterpillars, it will usually avoid other Monarchs.

**SOLITARY FEEDER**
The caterpillar of the Great Eggfly, a species of butterfly found in Asia and in the Pacific region, feeds on a range of plants as diverse as mallow and types of daisy. Adult Great Eggflies often mimic distasteful species of butterfly in order to protect themselves (see pp. 56–57 on mimicry).

An adult female
Great Eggfly butterfly

*Caterpillar armed with long spines characteristic of Heliconiidae caterpillars*

Flambeau caterpillar

*"Warning" red stripes usually indicate a poisonous caterpillar*

**DISTASTEFUL GANG**
Among the most beautifully colored butterflies, Heliconiines (sometimes called longwings) occur in the southern United States, and Central and South America. Like all Heliconiines, the caterpillars of these two species feed on poisonous passionflower vines.

Great Eggfly,
*Hypolimnas bolina,*
(S. E. Asia and Australia)

An adult Postman butterfly

An adult Flambeau butterfly

**DANGEROUS GROUP**
It is thought that the caterpillars of the Sweet Oil butterfly, *Mechanitis polymnia* (S. America), absorb poisonous substances from the leaves of the deadly nightshade plants they feed on. Although the poisons are harmless to the caterpillar or adult butterfly, they are extremely distasteful to a bird or any other enemy.

*Postman caterpillar*

Postman,
*Heliconius melpomene*
(S. America)

Adult Sweet Oil butterfly

*Unlike many species of caterpillar, Sweet Oils like to feed in a group*

Common Mormon,
*Papilio polytes,*
(S. E. Asia)

**SWALLOWTAIL DEFENSE**
The caterpillars of many swallowtail butterflies have a Y-shaped organ behind their heads. When the caterpillar is disturbed, it thrusts out two fingerlike glands, like pushing out the fingers of a glove, that emit an unpleasant smell.

*Y-shaped organ, known as osmeterium, is behind the caterpillar's head but not visible in the photograph*

*Some swallowtail caterpillars rear up in a threatening manner if disturbed*

Sweet Oil,
*Mechanitis polymnia,*
(S. America)

*Continued on next page*

## RAISING YOUR OWN CATERPILLARS

Raising butterflies and moths has always been a popular way of introducing children to the "miracle of nature". From caterpillars collected in the wild, or from eggs obtained from the adult, the growth and development of caterpillars can be observed at close quarters (see pp. 62–63).

Adult Cracker butterfly

Common Sailer, *Neptis hylas* (Asia)

## BABY CRACKERS

The species of *Hamadryas*, variously known as Calico, Click, or Cracker butterflies, are the only butterflies that make a sound as they fly. Their characteristic clicking noise is made by a special mechanism on the butterfly's wings.

*Cracker caterpillars have black head horns and long spines*

## DIFFERENT-COLORED CATERPILLARS

Even though they will retain their dead leaf camouflage throughout this stage of metamorphosis, these Common Sailer caterpillars go through a series of molts. By molting, a caterpillar not only increases its size, but also often alters its coloring and appearance.

## LEAVES ON LEAVES

Although the caterpillars of the Common Sailer butterfly may seem conspicuous on these individual leaves, in their natural setting their withered leaf camouflage blends in perfectly with the surrounding foliage.

Mixed group of Asian swallowtails include Common Mormon, *Papilio polytes;* Blue Mormon, *Papilio polymnestor;* Great Mormon, *Papilio memnon;* and Scarlet Swallowtail, *Papilio rumanzovia*

Common Sailer, *Neptis hylas* (Asia)

## SWARMING WITH SWALLOWTAILS

All the caterpillars on this plant are species of tropical *Papilio* or swallowtail butterflies. Because most of them are early stage larvae, it is difficult to identify individual species. The disguise taken on by this group resembles inedible bird droppings. This is obviously an extremely successful way of avoiding predatory birds.

Adult female Common Mormon butterfly

**A MOTH AMONG MANY**
Among the tropical caterpillars on these pages, the Silver-striped Hawkmoth is the only moth. For protection, it has a black horn at its end and a fearsome look, with large, yellow-ringed "eyes" on its back.

*Has the characteristic horn of hawkmoth caterpillars— really a harmless long spine*

Silver-striped Hawkmoth, *Hippotion celerio* (Europe, Africa, Asia, and Australia)

Adult Silver-striped Hawkmoth

Leopard, *Phalanta phalantha* (Africa and Asia)

Cracker, *Hamadryas amphinome* (C. and S. America)

Cracker, *Hamadryas feronia* (C. and S. America, sometimes Texas)

**LEOPARDS WITHOUT SPOTS**
Although this African species of butterfly doesn't look very aggressive, the popular name for it is the Leopard. Like the *Heliconius* caterpillars on pages 16 and 17, Leopards are members of the Nymphalid family, recognizable at the caterpillar stage by their spiny appearance.

**MEAL FOR A LIZARD**
Although it looks as though it is about to fall victim to a hungry lizard, the caterpillar may still be able to escape if it is distasteful or spiny. It might even drop to the ground to escape the lizard.

Cracker, (US Guatemalan Calico), *Hamadryas guatemalena* (C. America and sometimes Texas)

# Caterpillar to pupa

THE CATERPILLAR IS OFTEN REGARDED as simply the feeding stage in the life cycle of a butterfly, but it is a complex animal in its own right. It has to be capable of surviving in a hostile world, and it has to prepare for the vital transformation to the next, immobile stage, called the pupa, also known as the chrysalis (pp. 22–23). In moths, the chrysalis is normally contained within a cocoon (pp. 38–39). Scientists have performed experiments to show that this remarkable change is controlled by the insects' hormones. In normal circumstances, the caterpillar must look for a place to pupate. For example, this could be a site surrounded by foliage if the insect relies on concealment for protection. Alternatively, the chrysalis may be protected because it is distasteful to predators, so that concealment is not necessary.

Some caterpillars and chrysalises hang straight down without the support of a silken girdle. The skin splits along the caterpillar's back

Some species use their silk thread to bind together leaves for protection

**1 FINDING A SITE**
The caterpillar of the Citrus Swallowtail butterfly, *Papilio thoas* (S. America), selects a suitable site to turn into a pupa. Its hind claspers grip the plant stem.

**LEAF ROLLERS**
For added safety, some species pupate inside a rolled-up leaf. If disturbed on the leaf, the caterpillar will drop down on a silken thread and climb back up on to the leaf when the danger has passed.

**5 SPLITTING AT THE SEAMS**
The caterpillar wriggles vigorously and its skin begins to split along its back. The new chrysalis skin beneath is beginning to show through.

*Skin starting to split*

*New chrysalis skin*

*Empty skin and legs of caterpillar*

**6 NEW SKIN FOR OLD**
The caterpillar's movements gradually force off its old skin. The chrysalis skin starts to harden as it is exposed to the air.

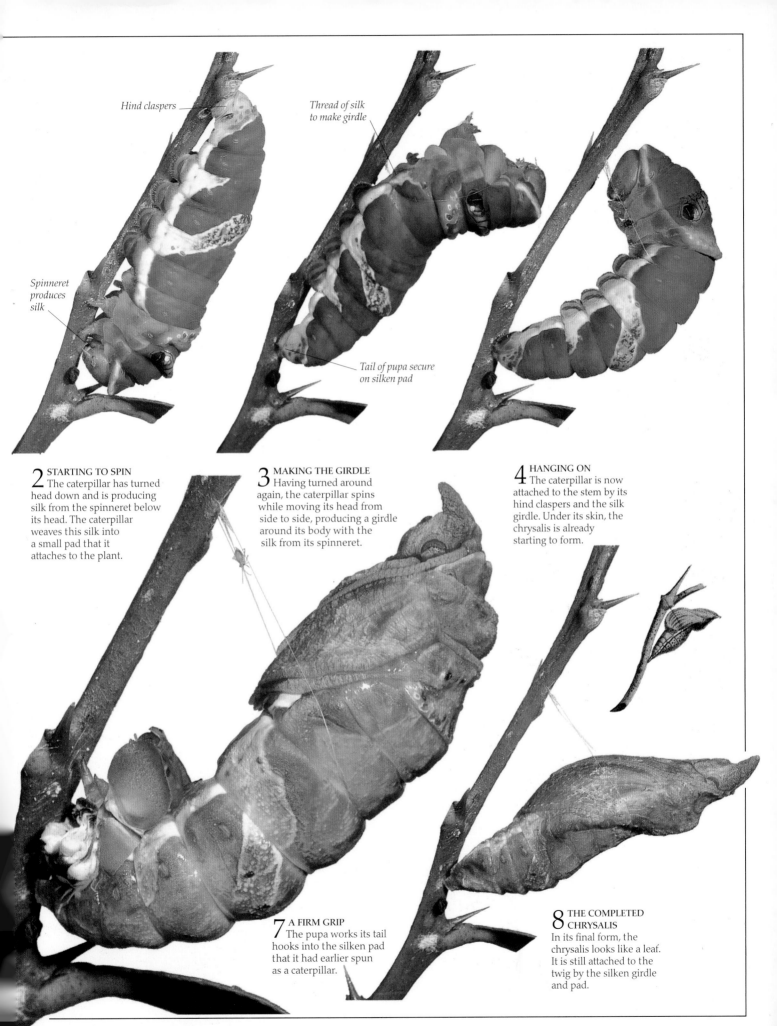

*Hind claspers*

*Spinneret produces silk*

*Thread of silk to make girdle*

*Tail of pupa secure on silken pad*

**2 STARTING TO SPIN**
The caterpillar has turned head down and is producing silk from the spinneret below its head. The caterpillar weaves this silk into a small pad that it attaches to the plant.

**3 MAKING THE GIRDLE**
Having turned around again, the caterpillar spins while moving its head from side to side, producing a girdle around its body with the silk from its spinneret.

**4 HANGING ON**
The caterpillar is now attached to the stem by its hind claspers and the silk girdle. Under its skin, the chrysalis is already starting to form.

**7 A FIRM GRIP**
The pupa works its tail hooks into the silken pad that it had earlier spun as a caterpillar.

**8 THE COMPLETED CHRYSALIS**
In its final form, the chrysalis looks like a leaf. It is still attached to the twig by the silken girdle and pad.

# The pupa stage

THE PUPA IS THE THIRD MAJOR STAGE in a butterfly or moth's life. This is when it is transformed from a caterpillar into an adult. A butterfly pupa is usually called a chrysalis and, depending on the species and climate, it remains in this form for weeks or even months. Except for an occasional twitch, the pupa seems lifeless, but, in fact, amazing changes are taking place, some of which can eventually be seen through the pupal skin. Because a pupa cannot move around, the insect is far more vulnerable to predators at this time than when it is a caterpillar or adult. For the majority of pupae, their best hope of survival is to adapt their shape and color to their surroundings. The exceptions are the more brightly colored pupae, which, being poisonous, are only too happy to advertise their presence. Many moths pupate underground, but few butterfly chrysalids have this added protection. Looking at the butterfly chrysalids on these pages, we can get some idea of how much they vary in shape and color.

**THE FREAK** *below*
As can be seen from these two *Calinaga buddha* (Asia) chrysalids, variation in color helps them to camouflage themselves on a wide range of backgrounds. The brown form will clearly have a protective advantage on a twig.

*Wing veins*

**THE ARCHDUKE** *left*
A close look reveals that the wing veins are visible, showing that the adult *Euthalia dirtea* (S. E. Asia) is almost ready to hatch.

**MALAY LACEWING** *below*
One of the important rules of camouflage is for the insect to break up its outline. The *Cethosia hypsea* (Asia) chrysalis does this by creating an irregular shape.

*Shaped like dead leaf for camouflage*

*Spiny shape for disguise*

**CRUISER** *left*
The resemblance to a dead and decaying leaf, and the spiny shape, helps protect *Vindula erota* (Asia) from detection by hungry predators.

*Bright reflective gold spot distracts predators*

*Visible wing veins*

**THE QUEEN** *above*
The chrysalis of *Danaus gilippus* (N., C. and S. America) is poisonous to predators. The poison comes from the plant on which the caterpillar feeds.

The swallowtail *Papilio machaon* (Europe, N. America, and Asia) is either green or brown.

**CRIMSON PATCH LONGWING** *left*
In addition to an irregular shape, *Heliconius erato* (S. America) has sharp spines along the wing case.

*Developing wing*

*Sharp spines*

**CLOUDLESS GIANT SULFUR** *right*
The green, leaflike shape of *Phoebis sennae* (N. and C. America) passes unnoticed in the vegetation of its natural habitat.

*Developing wing veins*

*Pronounced hump in middle*

An adult Cloudless Giant Sulfur (see above) beginning to break out of its chrysalis

*Developing head*

**POSTMAN**
Closely related to the Crimson Patch Longwing (left), the chrysalis of *Heliconius melpomene* (S. America) is equally well camouflaged and protective in shape.

**FLAMBEAU**
*Dryas julia* (C. and S. America) is another dark-brown, rugged-looking chrysalis that gains protection from its ability to resemble woody backgrounds.

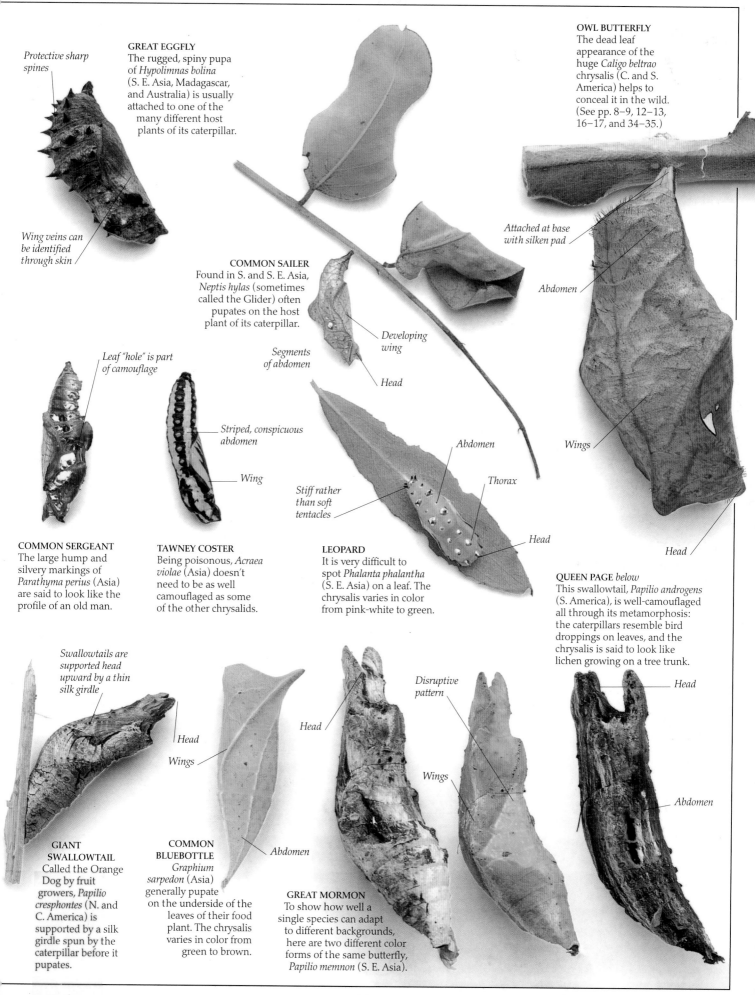

**Protective sharp spines**

**GREAT EGGFLY**
The rugged, spiny pupa of *Hypolimnas bolina* (S. E. Asia, Madagascar, and Australia) is usually attached to one of the many different host plants of its caterpillar.

**OWL BUTTERFLY**
The dead leaf appearance of the huge *Caligo beltrao* chrysalis (C. and S. America) helps to conceal it in the wild. (See pp. 8–9, 12–13, 16–17, and 34–35.)

**Wing veins can be identified through skin**

**COMMON SAILER**
Found in S. and S. E. Asia, *Neptis hylas* (sometimes called the Glider) often pupates on the host plant of its caterpillar.

**Attached at base with silken pad**

**Abdomen**

**Developing wing**

**Segments of abdomen**

**Head**

**Leaf "hole" is part of camouflage**

**Striped, conspicuous abdomen**

**Wing**

**Stiff rather than soft tentacles**

**Abdomen**

**Thorax**

**Head**

**Wings**

**Head**

**COMMON SERGEANT**
The large hump and silvery markings of *Parathyma perius* (Asia) are said to look like the profile of an old man.

**TAWNEY COSTER**
Being poisonous, *Acraea violae* (Asia) doesn't need to be as well camouflaged as some of the other chrysalids.

**LEOPARD**
It is very difficult to spot *Phalanta phalantha* (S. E. Asia) on a leaf. The chrysalis varies in color from pink-white to green.

**QUEEN PAGE** *below*
This swallowtail, *Papilio androgens* (S. America), is well-camouflaged all through its metamorphosis: the caterpillars resemble bird droppings on leaves, and the chrysalis is said to look like lichen growing on a tree trunk.

**Swallowtails are supported head upward by a thin silk girdle**

**Head**

**Wings**

**Head**

**Disruptive pattern**

**Head**

**Wings**

**Head**

**GIANT SWALLOWTAIL**
Called the Orange Dog by fruit growers, *Papilio cresphontes* (N. and C. America) is supported by a silk girdle spun by the caterpillar before it pupates.

**COMMON BLUEBOTTLE**
*Graphium sarpedon* (Asia) generally pupate on the underside of the leaves of their food plant. The chrysalis varies in color from green to brown.

**Abdomen**

**GREAT MORMON**
To show how well a single species can adapt to different backgrounds, here are two different color forms of the same butterfly, *Papilio memnon* (S. E. Asia).

**Wings**

**Abdomen**

# An emerging butterfly

As it changes from an egg to an adult, a butterfly renews itself on several different occasions. When the growing stages (metamorphosis) are over, all that remains is for the chrysalis to crack open and the adult to emerge. Within the virtually immobile chrysalis, such tremendous changes have taken place that when this happens a new creature appears to be born. The emerging butterfly shown here is a Blue Morpho, *Morpho peleides*, from Central and South America.

"The Flight into Egypt," from an illuminated manuscript, the *Hastings Hours*, c. 1480

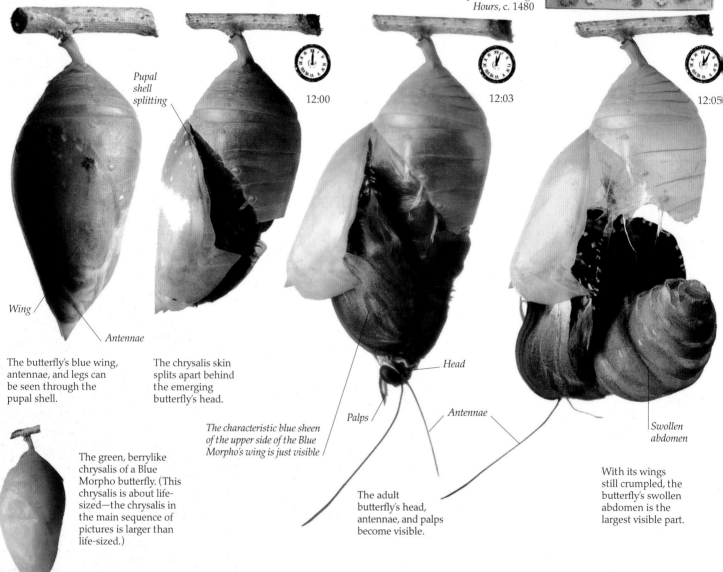

*Pupal shell splitting*

12:00

12:03

12:05

*Wing*

*Antennae*

The butterfly's blue wing, antennae, and legs can be seen through the pupal shell.

The chrysalis skin splits apart behind the emerging butterfly's head.

*The characteristic blue sheen of the upper side of the Blue Morpho's wing is just visible*

*Palps*

*Head*

*Antennae*

The green, berrylike chrysalis of a Blue Morpho butterfly. (This chrysalis is about life-sized—the chrysalis in the main sequence of pictures is larger than life-sized.)

The adult butterfly's head, antennae, and palps (sensory organs for tasting food) become visible.

*Swollen abdomen*

With its wings still crumpled, the butterfly's swollen abdomen is the largest visible part.

## 1 READY TO HATCH
Hours before emerging, the butterfly is still developing. By now, some of the Blue Morpho's structures can be seen through the skin of the chrysalis. The dark area is the butterfly's wing, and traces of the antennae and legs, are visible toward the bottom of the chrysalis. It takes about 85 days after the egg is laid for a Blue Morpho adult to emerge.

## 2 FIRST STAGE
Once the insect has completed its metamorphosis and is ready to emerge, it begins to pump body fluids into its head and thorax. This helps to split the chrysalis along certain weak points, so that the adult insect can begin to force its way out with its legs.

## 3 HEAD AND THORAX EMERGE
Once the skin of the chrysalis is broken, expansion can proceed more rapidly. Inflation is due not only to the body fluids in the head and thorax, but also to the air the insect takes in. Although by now the antennae, head, and palps (sensory organs for tasting food) are visible, the wings are still too soft and crumpled for identification.

## 4 COMPLETELY FREE
Having pushed its way out of the chrysalis, the butterfly's body now hangs free. At this stage, the butterfly's exoskeleton (the outside skeleton of all insects) is soft and still capable of more expansion. If, for any reason, the butterfly is damaged at this stage, or confined (perhaps by a thoughtless collector), complete expansion is not possible: all the parts harden and an injured butterfly results.

24

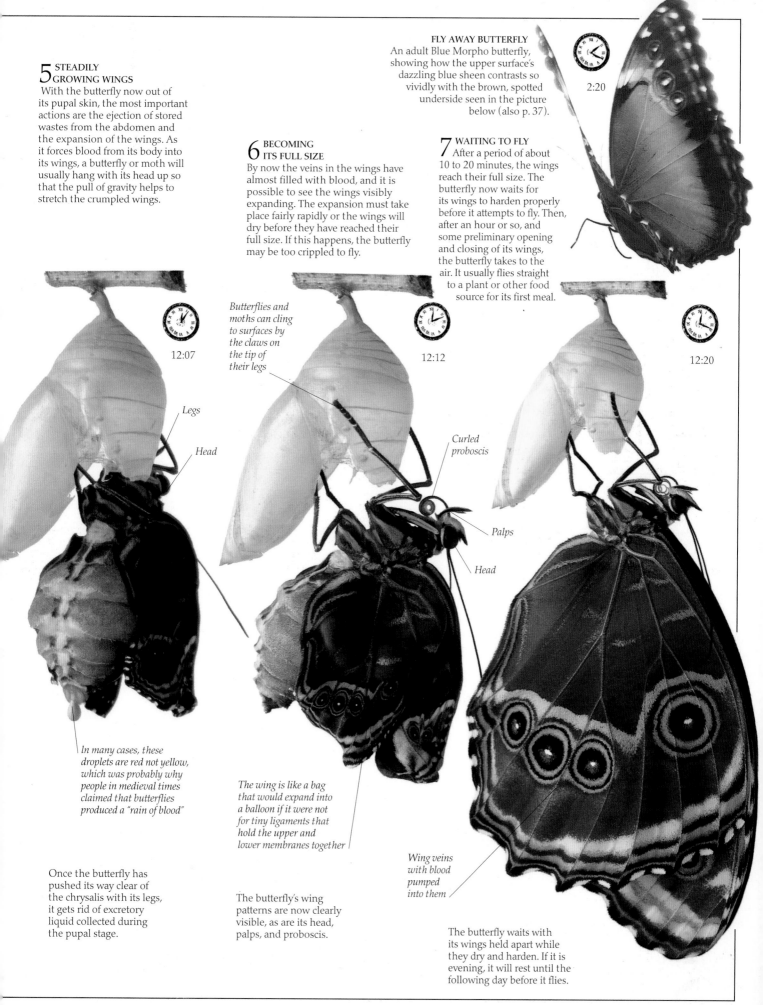

## 5 STEADILY GROWING WINGS

With the butterfly now out of its pupal skin, the most important actions are the ejection of stored wastes from the abdomen and the expansion of the wings. As it forces blood from its body into its wings, a butterfly or moth will usually hang with its head up so that the pull of gravity helps to stretch the crumpled wings.

## 6 BECOMING ITS FULL SIZE

By now the veins in the wings have almost filled with blood, and it is possible to see the wings visibly expanding. The expansion must take place fairly rapidly or the wings will dry before they have reached their full size. If this happens, the butterfly may be too crippled to fly.

## 7 WAITING TO FLY

After a period of about 10 to 20 minutes, the wings reach their full size. The butterfly now waits for its wings to harden properly before it attempts to fly. Then, after an hour or so, and some preliminary opening and closing of its wings, the butterfly takes to the air. It usually flies straight to a plant or other food source for its first meal.

**FLY AWAY BUTTERFLY**
An adult Blue Morpho butterfly, showing how the upper surface's dazzling blue sheen contrasts so vividly with the brown, spotted underside seen in the picture below (also p. 37).

2:20

12:07

*Butterflies and moths can cling to surfaces by the claws on the tip of their legs*

Legs

Head

Curled proboscis

Palps

Head

12:12

12:20

*In many cases, these droplets are red not yellow, which was probably why people in medieval times claimed that butterflies produced a "rain of blood"*

*The wing is like a bag that would expand into a balloon if it were not for tiny ligaments that hold the upper and lower membranes together*

*Wing veins with blood pumped into them*

Once the butterfly has pushed its way clear of the chrysalis with its legs, it gets rid of excretory liquid collected during the pupal stage.

The butterfly's wing patterns are now clearly visible, as are its head, palps, and proboscis.

The butterfly waits with its wings held apart while they dry and harden. If it is evening, it will rest until the following day before it flies.

# Butterflies

BUTTERFLIES AND MOTHS are unique among insects in that every part of their bodies, from their wings to their feet, is covered by thousands of delicate scales. The most noticeable scales are those covering the upper and under surfaces of the wings, since these give the butterfly its color and pattern. The head has two jointed sensory organs called antennae, used for smelling, and a specialized coiled feeding tube, or proboscis, that uncoils when the insect wishes to feed. The two large compound eyes are made up of many individual lenses, or facets. The facets are sensitive not only to movement, but also to the color patterns of flowers and other butterflies. Divided into three segments, the thorax is the powerhouse of the body, with connecting muscles for the two pairs of wings and the three pairs of segmented legs. The insect's reproductive organs are in the tip of the abdomen, the rest of which contains most of its digestive system.

A Clouded Yellow, *Colias croceus* (Europe), in flight

## Feeding habits

All butterflies and most moths have a proboscis (hollow feeding tube) used for drawing up energy-rich nectar, water, and other liquids. A few large moths do not feed as adults but live on food stored up by the larva (pp. 36–37). There are species of butterfly that enjoy sipping the juice of rotting fruit or the sap oozing from trees; others eat honey dew secreted by aphids, or the liquids from dead animal carcasses.

Labial palps (sensory feelers for testing food suitability)

Front of head

*Proboscis*

These insects belong to one of the largest and most colorful butterfly families, the Nymphalidae.

Close-up of the head of a Pearl-bordered Fritillary, *Clossiana euphrosyne* (Europe)

Compound eye

Labial palps

*Antenna*

*Coiled proboscis*

"TONGUE" SECTION *above*
A magnified cross section of the proboscis. Situated underneath the head, this hollow feeding tube acts like a tightly coiled drinking straw.

A DRINK AT THE CLUB
It is a very common sight, especially in hot climates, to see a group of male butterflies drinking from damp soil—possibly to obtain minerals. The majority of the butterflies in this "mud-puddle" club are Bluebottles, *Graphium sarpedon*, from Malaysia.

## HOMERUS SWALLOWTAIL, *PAPILIO HOMERUS* (JAMAICA)

Forewing

Hind wing

**RESTING POSITION** *left*
In this old engraving, a Scarce Swallowtail, *Iphiclides podalirius* (Europe & Asia), is shown in a typical swallowtail resting position, with its wings folded above its body.

Head

Thorax

Abdomen

**MAGNIFIED SCALES**
A close-up view of the eyespot of a South American butterfly reveals the overlapping scales that form the wing pattern. In this picture, the tough wing veins are clearly visible.

**WHICH FAMILY?**
The veins in the wings of butterflies and moths help to keep the wing in the correct flight position. The way the veins are arranged also helps identify which family of butterflies or moths a species belongs to.

**COMING IN TO LAND**
With its wings slightly curved, a Peacock butterfly, *Inachis io* (Europe), is about to land on a buddleia. Butterflies have such control over their flight movements that they can make sudden landings.

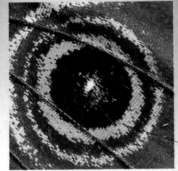

*Rows of scales form the beautiful patterns and colors of butterfly wings*

# Temperate butterflies

"TEMPERATE" IS HOW WE DESCRIBE the regions of the Earth with warm summers and cold winters. In these temperate areas, butterflies are inactive during the winter months and so must be able to survive without feeding. Winter is often passed in the chrysalis stage, but there are a few butterflies in Europe and North America that pass the winter as adults, hibernating until the warmer spring weather (p. 51). The wide variety of flowers in temperate meadows and woodland clearings means that there are plenty of butterflies, although not as many as in the tropics (pp. 32–35). Temperate habitats have been increasingly destroyed and developed during recent years, and consequently butterflies are becoming less common. Their disappearance is especially sad because for most of us butterflies are the spirit of summer. Indeed, the term "butterfly" may well come from "butter-colored fly," a name for the yellow-colored Brimstone, which is one of the first European butterflies to appear each summer.

The Peacock, *Inachis io*, is one of the most common and distinctive butterflies in Europe and temperate Asia

An old engraving of a Small Copper (right) and (probably) a female Common Blue (Europe)

**DISAPPEARING COPPER**
Land drainage has resulted in the gradual disappearance of the Large Copper, *Lycaena dispar*, from marshy areas of Central Europe and temperate Asia (p. 58).

## Grassland butterflies

**GRASSLAND HABITAT**
Species of butterfly whose caterpillars feed on grasses are found in meadows, heathlands, and the edges of woodlands and rivers.

**BEAUTIFUL BLUE**
In Europe, the Adonis Blue, *Lysandra bellargus*, is threatened in areas where its grassland habitat is no longer grazed by rabbits or sheep. It is now protected by law in France.

**BENEFITING EACH OTHER**
Caterpillars of the Large Blue, *Maculinea arion* (Europe), live in ants' nests, where they feed on the ant larvae. The caterpillars are not attacked by the ants, who milk them for a sugary solution (p. 58).

**BROUGHT UP ON VIOLETS**
The Aphrodite, *Speyeria aphrodite*, is found in the grasslands and open woodlands of western North America. The caterpillars feed on violets.

**BROWN, OR BLACK-AND-WHITE?**
Although belonging to the Satyridae family, or "browns", the Marbled White, *Melanargia galathea* (Europe and Asia), has a black-and-white pattern.

**SUCCESSFUL BROWN**
The Meadow Brown, *Maniola jurtina* (Europe, Asia, and Africa) is a typical, well-camouflaged grassland butterfly.

*This butterfly probably gets its name because it enjoys basking on walls with its wings outspread*

**SUN LOVER**
The Wall butterfly, *Lasiommata megera* (Europe, Asia, and N. Africa), is another grass-feeding species.

*Somber colors on the upper and underside provide good camouflage*

**WIDESPREAD IN EUROPE**
Although most coppers occur in Asia and America, the Purple-shot Copper, *Heodes alciphron*, is European.

**A COMMON CRESCENTSPOT**
The Field Crescentspot, *Phyciodes campestris*, is common in the uplands of western North America.

# Woodland butterflies

### GREEN CAMOUFLAGE
With its brown top side and beautiful green underside, the Green Hairsteak, *Callophrys rubi* (Europe, Asia, and N. Africa), has ideal woodland camouflage.

### FROM COMMA TO HOP
The Comma, also popularly known as the Hop Merchant, *Polygonia comma*, is found in a wide range of woodlands in North America and Europe. It belongs to a group of butterflies called anglewings, in which different species have been named after their distinctive wing markings.

*Irregular dead-leaf outline and pattern gives effective camouflage*

Top side of Comma

*The name "Comma" refers to a mark on the underside of the hind wing*

Underside of Comma

Oak leaves

*Hairstreaks are usually dark on the top, with different color variations on the underside*

### MIXED WOODLAND HABITAT
Because of the variety of food sources, more species of butterfly are found in mixed woodland than in any other habitat. Some species of butterfly can be found flying at a low level in shady woodland clearings, while others live high among the treetops. Other species of butterfly live along woodland edges, and in areas where people have cleared forests.

### IN STREAMS TO CANYONS
The Acadian Hairstreak, *Satyrium acadica* (N. America), occurs in damp meadows, by streams, and in canyons.

### OAK FOREST RESIDENT
The Purple Hairstreak, *Quercusia quercus*, is one of a number of European and Asian species of hairstreaks.

*This is the form from southern Europe—the Speckled Wood in northern Europe has creamy-white markings*

*Only males have shimmering wing scales that reflect purple when the light is at a particular angle*

### BROKEN PATTERN
The color pattern of the Common Glider, *Neptis sappho* (Europe and Asia), is less noticeable in the dappled light of a woodland glade.

### WOODLAND CAMOUFLAGE
The color pattern of the Speckled Wood, *Pararge aegeria* (Europe, Asia, and N. Africa), makes it especially difficult to spot in patches of sunlight.

### FEEDS ON DEAD ANIMALS
Although the Purple Emperor, *Apatura iris* (Europe and Asia), flies high up in trees, the males are attracted to the ground to feed on rotting animal carcasses.

*Pine White caterpillars sometimes completely strip pine trees of their leaves*

### INTO THE WOOD
The Woodland Grayling, *Hipparchia fagi* (Europe and Asia), blends with bark patterns on tree trunks.

### PINE PEST
The adult Pine White, *Neophasia menapia* (N. America), lives among the pine trees on which its caterpillars feed.

### FLYING TORTOISES
Large Tortoiseshells, *Nymphalis polychloros* (Europe and Asia), often occur in wooded uplands.

# Mountain butterflies

Of all the environments in which butterflies and moths live, the short summers, cold nights, and strong winds of the mountains and Arctic tundra are surely the most hostile. Insects have to adapt to survive harsh climates, which is why many mountain butterflies are darker than related species from lowland areas. Because darker colors absorb sunlight more easily, the insects can warm up rapidly in the early morning when the air temperature is low. Other mountain and Arctic butterflies retain heat through the long, hairy scales that cover their bodies. The rocky terrain of high mountains causes many species to lay their eggs in rocky crevices rather than on plants, while the short summer season means that they can only breed once a year. Butterflies living in constant strong winds fly in low, short bursts to keep from being blown away, and many flatten themselves against rocks when at rest. Although few species are found at very high altitudes, there are notable exceptions of intrepid butterflies living on the edge of the snow line in mountain ranges such as the Himalayas.

*Short antennae and long, hairlike body scales of all Parnassius butterflies*

Small Apollo, *Parnassius phoebus* (Europe, Asia, and N. America)

### HIGH FLIER
The beautiful Apollo, *Parnassius apollo*, is found on some of the higher mountains of Europe and Asia. It is now protected in most of Europe because its many local forms are much sought after by collectors.

Male     Female

Although not a mountain species, the female Mottled Umber, *Erannis defoliara*, is wingless

### FLIGHTLESS MOTHER
Some moths have wingless females, which can be an advantage on mountains where a moth could be blown away while laying its eggs.

Top side of a Hermit butterfly

Underside of a Hermit butterfly

### STONY SURVIVOR
One of the best ways for a butterfly to survive in a bare, rocky environment is to be well camouflaged at all times. The Hermit butterfly, *Chazara briseis*, can be found on dry stony slopes in central and southern Europe and the Middle East.

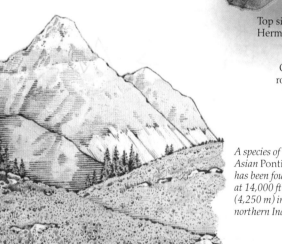

### HIGH MOUNTAIN HABITAT
Butterflies and moths are attracted to Alpine meadows by the numerous summer flowers. This scene could be in the American Rockies, the European Alps, or the Asian Himalayas.

*A species of Asian* Pontia *has been found at 14,000 ft (4,250 m) in northern India*

### CLOSE TO THE SNOW LINE
The Peak White butterfly, *Pontia callidice* (Europe and Asia), a relative of the Western White, *Pontia occidentalis* (N. America), is found near the snow line on high alpine mountains.

### FRIEND OR ENEMY?
Found on higher ground in mainland Europe and Asia, the caterpillar of the Idas Blue, *Lycaeides idas*, spends the winter in ants' nests. The higher the altitude, the smaller this tiny butterfly becomes.

### HIGH OR LOW
While Zephyr Blue, *Plebejus pylaon*, colonies are found in a variety of grassy habitats in Europe and Asia; the subspecies *trappi* occurs only in the central and southern European highlands.

**MARSHES TO MOUNTAINS**
During the short Arctic summer, the Moorland Clouded Yellow (US Palaeno Sulfur), *Colias palaeno*, occurs in North America, Europe, and Asia in marshy and mountain areas.

**ROCKY MOUNTAIN VISITOR**
The Piedmont Ringlet, *Erebia meolans*, is often seen on the rocky slopes of southern Europe. A number of related species of *Erebia* occur in the mountains of North America.

**NOT SCARCE BUT NOT THERE**
Once believed to occur in Britain, the Scarce Copper, *Heodes virgaureae*, in fact only occurs in the mountainous areas of central Europe.

**MOUNTAIN FLOWERS**
Butterflies and moths flourish in the wild Alpine pastures, where few people go. Heather (below) is typical of the plants that attract mountain and tundra butterflies in high summer.

**WAY OUT WEST**
Although the Northern Marblewing, *Euchloe creusa*, comes from the mountains of the American West, it has several European relatives. Its name comes from the pattern on its hind wings.

**DIFFICULT TO FIND**
Cynthia's Fritillary, *Euphydryas cynthia*, only occurs in the European Alps and the mountains of Bulgaria. There are many species of fritillary, both in North America and Europe.

**MOUNTAIN BEAUTY**
The striking Bhutan Glory, *Bhutanitis lidderdalei*, comes from the mountain forests of Thailand and India. In Thailand, many of these butterflies are killed and exported to collectors.

*Prominent tails on hind wings distract birds from pecking at more vulnerable parts of the body*

*Large eyespots can startle predatory birds*

**ONE OF A KIND**
Butler's Mountain White, *Baltia butleri*, comes from the Himalayas. There are similar species of mountain whites in South America.

# Exotic butterflies

NO REGION HAS SO MANY marvelously colored and patterned butterflies as the tropics—the hot areas of the Earth that are near the equator. The range of color and pattern is quite remarkable, although we can only guess why some of these butterflies are so brightly colored. It may be for display to attract a mate, but equally it may be a form of camouflage. In the bright tropical forest, with its deep shadows and intense patches of sunlight, a brightly colored butterfly may not be conspicuous. In many species, the bright colors warn predators that the butterflies are distasteful. But, however wide a range of color and pattern tropical butterflies display, they are less variable in shape than moths. There are also far fewer species of butterfly than moth in the world.

*Trailing tails typical of many swallowtails*

**FOREST MYSTERY** *above*
Since it lives high up in the dense, steamy forests of New Guinea, it is not surprising that little is known about the Purple Spotted Swallowtail, *Graphium weiskei*.

*Unusually shaped wings measure 5 in (13 cm) across*

**BRILLIANT GREEN BEAUTY**
Some of the loveliest butterflies are the large birdwing swallowtails of the New Guinea region. Species such as the *Ornithoptera priamus* are protected from overselling, but not from the destruction of their habitat.

*Males of priamus group of birdwings have golden fringes on hind wings for transferring scent during courtship*

**TROPICAL RAINFOREST HABITAT**
Although tropical rainforests can be found in Southeast Asia, North-east Australia, the South Pacific islands, and Central Africa, the place to look for the widest range of tropical butterflies is Central and South America. In these impenetrable areas, with no winter, abundant rainfall, and a huge variety of plants, butterflies have the perfect living quarters.

**WET OR DRY** *below*
When it flies, the highly visible Mother of Pearl, *Protogoniomorpha parhassus* (Africa), catches the light. But once at rest in the rainforest, its color and shape make it look like a dead leaf. Mother of Pearls have wet and dry season forms—in the wet season, the butterflies are smaller than in the dry season.

**SPECTACULAR SWALLOWTAIL**
The striking Cattle Heart Swallowtail, *Parides eurimedes*, is still quite common in parts of Central and South America. It can be seen from sea level to 5,000 ft (1,500 m), flying along the edges of rainforests.

*Tail-less swallowtail*

*Irregularly shaped wing*

## CAMOUFLAGE BAND
Very little is known about the conspicuous-looking *Taenaris schoenbergi* (New Guinea). It is likely that the band across its forewings is a form of camouflage, concealing the true outline of the butterfly when it is resting.

The waxy green leaves and brilliant red flowers of a hanging *Columnia* are typical of tropical plants (right)

*Camouflage band across forewing*

## DISTRACTING TAILS *below*
Species of swallowtail with distinctive trailing tails are known as "clubtails". The Yellow-bodied Clubtail, *Atrophaneura neptunus*, lives in the humid forests of Malaysia.

*Conspicious, red spot on hind wing distracts predators from attacking the butterfly's body*

## BUTTERFLY FEEDING
A 19th-century painting by Marianne North of an exotic-looking butterfly feeding on nutmeg juices in Jamaica.

## BRIGHT TEMPTRESS
Jezebel is the popular name for several species of *Delias* butterfly. *Delias belisama* flies in the mountainous areas of Indonesia, where its beautiful bright orange color can easily be spotted in the damp, misty tropical forests.

## ROYAL ROAD RUNNER
If you could find the rare Royal Assyrian, *Terinos clarissa*, it would be flying at low altitudes near roadsides, quarries, and rocky outcrops in Malaysia and Indonesia. The caterpillar is covered with long, branched spines.

## KEEPING OUT OF SIGHT *right*
Little is known about the rare *Dynastor napoleon*, except that it probably flies only at dusk in the rainforests of Brazil. Since the underside of the huge wing is patterned like a leaf, the butterfly is well camouflaged at rest.

## LIZARD ENEMY
Tropical butterflies need defense mechanisms, such as trailing tails, frightening eyespots, and poisonous scales to escape from predators such as lizards.

*Continued on next page*

**MORE COLORFUL MALE**
A collector brought this nymphalid butterfly, *Myscelia orsis*, back from Paraguay many years ago. The vivid blue of this male contrasts sharply with the duller and more strongly patterned female.

**NOT REALLY A MIMIC** *right*
The male Danaid Eggfly looks very different from the female (below). Other popular names for this species, found in Africa, N. and C. America, India, and Australia, are the Mimic, Diadem, or Six-continents.

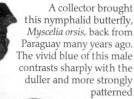

Male butterfly

**PART OF A GROUP** *below*
The Theclid Hairstreak, *Amblypodia morphina*, is one of a number of similar Southeast Asian butterflies. A female from this group would be paler in color than this male.

Female butterfly

Butterfly's underside—top side has plainer brown forewing with broad white band

**PERFECT LOOK-ALIKE** *above*
The nonpoisonous female Danaid Eggfly, *Hypolimnas misippus*, is a brilliant impersonator of the poisonous Tiger butterfly, *Danaus chrysippus* (See mimicry, pp. 56–57).

**BRIGHT UNDERWINGS** *right*
Like many butterflies, the underside (illustrated) of the Malay Lacewing, *Cethosia hypsaea*, has a more interesting pattern than the top side. This specimen was collected in Borneo.

Bright red pattern is typical of a poisonous butterfly's warning colors

An engraving of a tropical swallowtail, *Papilio crino* (Sri Lanka)

Characteristic large wings of many swallowtails

**POISONOUS GIANT**
A wingspan of up to 10 in (25 cm) makes the African Giant Swallowtail, *Papilio antimachus*, the largest African butterfly. The butterfly is believed to be extremely poisonous and is avoided by its enemies in the rainforest.

**BEAT THIS CAMOUFLAGE** *below*
Few butterflies have a more interesting resting camouflage than the South American butterfly *Coenophlebia archidona*.

Underside looks like a dead leaf

Large eyespot for startling predators

**BANANA EATER** *left*
The adults of *Taenaris macrops* (New Guinea) like feeding on ripe bananas. The caterpillars of some *Taenaris* butterflies feed on banana leaves.

Silvery patches imitate the fungi found on dead leaves

*Continued from previous page*

*Broken pattern camouflage*

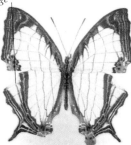

## MYSTERY MAP-WING
Although the Map-winged butterfly, *Cyrestis nivea,* is common in Malaysia and Indonesia, very little is known about its habits. Its broken pattern certainly gives it a formidable protective camouflage.

## ATTENTION-SEEKER *below*
The easily recognizable Ruddy Daggerwing, *Marpesia petreus,* can be seen in woods and thickets in the southern United States, and Central and South America.

## RAINFOREST DAZZLER
The group of South American butterflies called *Morphos* include some of the world's most dazzling butterflies (also pp. 24–25). The wings of species such as *Morpho cypris* are often used for jewelry.

*Morpho butterflies are camouflaged by their brown underwings*

*Long tails on hind wings distract would-be predators from attacking body, or the main part of the wings*

*Underside of male—the top side is mostly white with a darker margin*

## MORPHO WING PENDANT
It is argued that the collection of millions of *Morpho* butterflies to use as jewelry does not affect the population, since only males are collected. Female *Morphos* are not only less dazzling, but also much shyer, making them difficult to catch in their rainforest habitats.

## "A COLLECTOR AT WORK"
In the 1920s, Arthur Twidle painted a number of scenes to illustrate his book, *Beautiful Butterflies of the Tropics.*

*This exotic lily is called a Peace Lily*

## DULL ON TOP
Like other *Delias* butterflies, the Imperial White, *Delias harpalyce* (S. E. Australia) is unusual in having a more brightly colored underside than top side.

*Method of setting a butterfly (below)*

Oblong collecting box, lined at the top and bottom with cork

## OWL'S HEAD
The huge South American Owl butterfly gets its name from the owllike eyespots on the underside of the wings. Many birds will understandably keep away from anything resembling an owl. This species, *Caligo prometheus,* lives in the rainforests of Ecuador and Colombia.

*Eyespot on underside of Owl butterfly's hind wings shown on pp. 8–9*

Since they dislike bright sunshine, Owl butterflies fly in dark places, or at dusk

# Moths

THERE ARE AT LEAST 150,000 DIFFERENT SPECIES of moth, compared with some 17,000 butterfly species. *Nachtschmetterlinge* ("night butterflies"), the German word for moths, clearly reflects the popular view of their behavior. While it is true that the majority of moths fly at dusk or during the night, quite a large number are day-fliers (pp. 48–49). Although moths such as the silkworm (pp. 40–41) are useful to humans, a few species of moth are harmful. These include the moths that destroy crops, fruits, or trees; the clothes moths that damage woolen goods; and moths that spread diseases in cattle by feeding on the moisture around their eyes (p. 56). The majority of moths are harmless, pollinating flowers and forming a vital part of the complex web of life.

An engraving showing the main parts of a moth, with the darker lines representing the fascia, which are part of the wing pattern

**THE LONGEST TONGUE?**
This amazing proboscis belongs to Darwin's Hawkmoth, *Xanthopan morganii,* from Madagascar. Charles Darwin, the celebrated 19th-century English naturalist, knew of an orchid in which the nectar was at the base of a 12 in (30 cm) corolla. Since the orchid obviously needed to be pollinated, Darwin thought there must be a moth with a proboscis between 12 and 13 in (30 to 35 cm). Years later, the discovery of this hawkmoth proved that Darwin's theory was correct.

## Feeding

Like butterflies, most moths take nectar from flowers. You may be able to see day-flying moths (pp. 48–49) hovering in front of a flower as they feed. Many large moths do not feed at all as adults. During its short adult life, the Indian Moon moth (right and below) lives entirely off food stored in its body during the caterpillar stage.

**FINDING NECTAR** *below right*
The long proboscis of this hawkmoth seeks out nectar from flowers. During this probing, pollen is picked up and transferred from flower to flower.

*Characteristic thick body and long forewings of all hawkmoths. All the moths in this group are powerful fliers*

The head has the cerebral ganglion ("brain") inside. The eyes, antennae, and sense organs, called palps, give the insect information about its environment.

*Antenna*

*Maxillary palp*

*Labial palp*

*Eye*

*Proboscis*

*Labial palp*

**FACE-TO-FACE WITH A MOTH**
An almost head-on view of the Indian Moon moth shows its antennae, and front and middle legs. The antennae have tiny sense organs that probably detect not only scent but also changes in air pressure.

*The female Moon moth uses its antennae to select the correct food plant on which to lay its eggs*

*Since this moth does not feed as an adult, it has no proboscis*

*Trailing tails help to protect the moth*

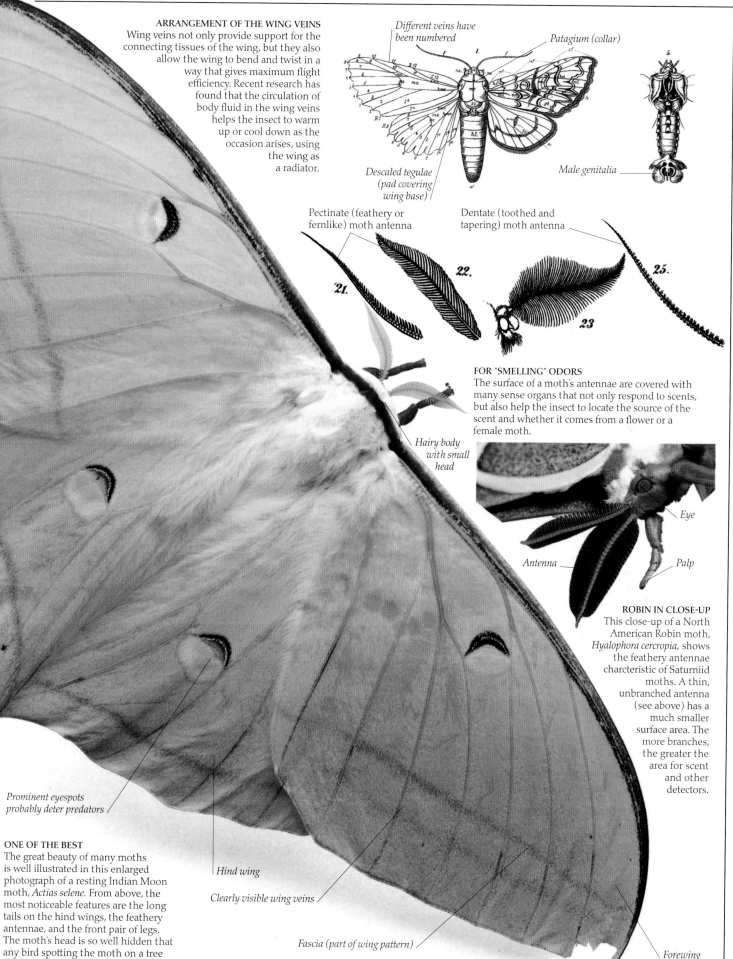

**ARRANGEMENT OF THE WING VEINS**
Wing veins not only provide support for the connecting tissues of the wing, but they also allow the wing to bend and twist in a way that gives maximum flight efficiency. Recent research has found that the circulation of body fluid in the wing veins helps the insect to warm up or cool down as the occasion arises, using the wing as a radiator.

*Different veins have been numbered*

*Patagium (collar)*

*Descaled tegulae (pad covering wing base)*

*Male genitalia*

*Pectinate (feathery or fernlike) moth antenna*

*Dentate (toothed and tapering) moth antenna*

*21.*

*22.*

*23.*

*25.*

**FOR "SMELLING" ODORS**
The surface of a moth's antennae are covered with many sense organs that not only respond to scents, but also help the insect to locate the source of the scent and whether it comes from a flower or a female moth.

*Hairy body with small head*

*Eye*

*Antenna*

*Palp*

**ROBIN IN CLOSE-UP**
This close-up of a North American Robin moth, *Hyalophora cercropia,* shows the feathery antennae charcteristic of Saturniid moths. A thin, unbranched antenna (see above) has a much smaller surface area. The more branches, the greater the area for scent and other detectors.

*Prominent eyespots probably deter predators*

**ONE OF THE BEST**
The great beauty of many moths is well illustrated in this enlarged photograph of a resting Indian Moon moth, *Actias selene.* From above, the most noticeable features are the long tails on the hind wings, the feathery antennae, and the front pair of legs. The moth's head is so well hidden that any bird spotting the moth on a tree will probably peck at the long tails.

*Hind wing*

*Clearly visible wing veins*

*Fascia (part of wing pattern)*

*Forewing*

# Cocoons

MOST MOTHS SPIN A COCOON. This silk case encloses the caterpillar as it pupates and the inactive pupa while it is developing. Some species incorporate stinging hairs from the last caterpillar skin, or bits of plant material into the cocoon as added protection or camouflage. The development of cocoons reaches its peak in the silk moths (pp. 40–41), whose cocoons are made up of a single thread (sometimes about half a mile (800 m) long), wrapped around and around many times. When the adult moth is ready to emerge, it has to force its way out of the cocoon. This can be difficult, since the cocoon is often very hard. Some moths have a file-like organ with which to cut their way out; others produce a liquid that softens the walls. Many caterpillars also spin silk webs to protect themselves while they are feeding, although these are not true cocoons.

**HANGING BY A THREAD**
Some species suspend their cocoons from a long silk thread—an added protection against predatory insects.

**IN DISGUISE**
These silk moth cocoons look very much like a part of the plant from which they hang, safe from all but the most sharp-eyed predators.

**"WOODEN" COCOON**
This Green Silver-lines moth, *Bena fagana* (Europe), has just emerged. Its cocoon incorporated bits of bark chewed off by the caterpillar, to provide strength and camouflage.

*Large silk web extends across several leaves, giving the caterpillars plenty of room to move around and feed*

*Hard surface of cocoon, reinforced by fragments of bark*

**CATERPILLAR SHELTER**
Silk is used extensively by caterpillars. Many species of *Yponomeuta* moth spin a protective web and live communally under it, feeding on the plant. Some of the smaller caterpillars may get blown around and use the silk like a parachute.

*Distinctive wing pattern shows how the Green Silver-lines gets its name*

*Flimsy net helps to keep pupa in place*

**BURIED ALIVE**
Hawkmoths are one of the moth families that pupate below ground. The caterpillar makes a small cavity and spins silk around the walls. This helps to protect it from the damp as well as from animals burrowing in the soil.

**UNDERGROUND NET**
The pupae of the Silver-striped Hawkmoth, *Hippotion celerio* (Europe, Africa, and Asia; also p. 19), have a very flimsy cocoon, consisting of a few strands of silk woven into a net.

*These moths pupate underground*

*Caterpillar that has fallen off the web hanging on its own thread of silk*

**WILD SILK PRODUCERS**
The Oak Silk moth, *Antheraea harti* (Asia; see pp. 62–63), is one of a number of species of wild silk moths in the family Saturniidae. Its caterpillars feed on oak leaves, among which they also spin their cocoons. These moths are related to the Chinese silk moths that produce most commercial silk.

*Caterpillar starting to join leaves together with silk*

*Oak leaf partly eaten by caterpillar*

*Caterpillar eating oak leaf*

*Head of caterpillar*

**THE COCOON TAKES SHAPE**
The Oak Silk moth caterpillars are beginning to spin among the leaves near the top of the plant, and already the cocoon is starting to form. Eventually, they will spin large quantities of silk to make their cocoons.

*Network of silk threads forms "framework" of cocoon*

*Tail of caterpillar*

*Strong, hard covering of silk*

**COMPLETED COCOON**
The finished cocoon of the Oak Silk moth shows clearly how the leaves are bound together by a dense network of silk threads. These wild silk moth cocoons are used commercially but not on the scale of the silkworm, *Bombyx mori* (Asia; pp. 40–41).

*The silk moth caterpillars eat only leaves of the oak (Quercus robur) and not the acorns*

# Silk moths

VERMIS SERICVS.

Illustrations from *Vermis sericus*, a popular 17th-century book on silk moths

**S**ILK IS PRODUCED by most moth caterpillars; but the finest quality silk is made by species of moth in the families Saturniidae and Bombycidae and, in particular, by the caterpillars of the large white moth, *Bombyx mori* (Asia), popularly known as the silkworm. According to Chinese legend, silk fiber was first discovered in about 2700 BCE, but for centuries the methods used to produce silk commercially were kept a well-guarded secret—the export of silkworms or their eggs out of China was punishable by death. Eventually silkworm eggs, and the seeds of the mulberry trees the caterpillars feed on, were smuggled out of China, supposedly hidden in a cane. Silk continued to command high prices in Europe—even after the Arabs had introduced silkworms into Spain, and silk weaving centers had been started in Italy. Today, the silkworm has become so domesticated that it no longer occurs in the wild.

**SILK GOWNS**
For many years, silk has been a highly prized material for luxurious wedding dresses and evening gowns

**REELING OF THE COCOONS**
This 19th-century Chinese engraving shows the thread being transferred onto smaller bobbins. Today, silk-making is more mechanized, but the basic process remains the same.

**UNWINDING THE THREAD**
From its origins in China (above) to 17th-century Europe (below), the methods used to produce silk changed little. The insects inside the cocoons were killed in boiling water before they could hatch and break the thread of silk. The hot water also had the effect of dissolving the gumlike substance holding the strands together. The threads from several cocoons were then caught up, twisted together, and wound on a reel or frame.

**3 BUILDING UP THE WALLS**
The caterpillar has worked backward and forward between the leaves, making the cocoon thicker. All the time, the silk is being forced out through the caterpillar's spinneret.

In ancient China, the cocoon shells were opened after the silk was removed, and the caterpillar eaten

# 1 FINDING A SITE

The caterpillar of the silkworm, *Bombyx mori* (Asia), finds a suitable site surrounded by leaves before beginning to spin silk. This is produced by glands in the caterpillar's body and comes out through the spinneret under its head.

*Silk thread attached to surrounding leaves at many points*

# 2 THE EARLY STAGES

To start with, the caterpillar spins a small web, weaving the silk thread into a loose cocoon. At this point, the network of the cocoon is not very dense, so the caterpillar is still clearly visible.

*Nearly completed cocoon with dense walls of silk*

*Each cocoon is made of a single thread of silk that, when unraveled, is about 0.5 miles (800 m) long*

# 4 INCREASING THE INTENSITY

The thickness of the silk layer increases and the cocoon will now keep most parasites and predators away from the caterpillar.

# 5 A SAFE HAVEN

The cocoon is now strong enough to protect the caterpillar completely as it starts to pupate and, eventually, as it changes into a moth.

*Fully protected caterpillar can now begin to pupate*

# Temperate moths

TEMPERATE MOTHS, LIKE BUTTERFLIES from the same regions (pp. 28–29), have to be able to survive the cold winter months. While some temperate moths remain at the egg stage, others pass the winter as caterpillars, perhaps concealed inside the stem of a plant. Many more survive as a pupa, which in some species is further protected in a cocoon (pp. 38–39). In the temperate areas of Europe, Asia, and North America, a moth's life cycle is synchronized with the spring and summer months, when there are plenty of grasses and flowers. The greatest variety of temperate moths are found during warm summer nights, when they can be seen at windows, or flying around some other source of light. On a moonlit night, it may just be possible to see them sipping the nectar from flowers. Although most temperate moths fly only by night, certain species are active in the daytime (pp. 48–49).

*Female of species is white throughout; in the male, the upper surface of hind wing is yellow*

### MISNAMED MOTH *above*
Despite its name, the Salt-marsh moth, *Estigmene acrea*, occurs in a variety of habitats throughout North America and Mexico.

*Featherlike antenna*

*Wings have faded after death—originally pale green color*

*Adults do not feed*

### BEAUTIFUL SILK MOTH
The spectacular Luna moth, *Actias luna*, is found only in North America. In recent years, its numbers have decreased due to pollution and insecticides. Like the Indian Moon moth (pp. 36–37), it is often bred in captivity.

*Bright pattern warns predator that the moth is poisonous*

*Long tails on hind wings*

### POISONOUS TIGER *above*
Like other tiger moths, the Virgin Tiger moth, *Grammia virgo* (N. America), is avoided by birds because of its distasteful body fluids.

### HOLLOWING A HOME
The caterpillar of the Locust-bean moth, *Ectomyelois ceratoniae* (worldwide), pupates in hollowed-out thistle stems.

### PALER TIGER MOTH *right*
This day-flying Zuni Tiger, *Arachnis zuni*, can be found in the southwestern United States and Mexico. Like the Virgin Tiger (above), its color gives warning.

*Dull-colored forewings*

*When disturbed, the red hind wings are flashed to confuse predators*

### STARING EYES
The Eyed Hawkmoth, *Smennthus ocellata* (Europe and Asia), gets its name from the eyespots on its hind wings. If the moth is disturbed, it moves its forewings to reveal two large, staring "eyes."

*Eyespots scare enemies away*

### FRUIT EATER *left*
Because the caterpillar of the Codling moth, *Cydia pomonella* (worldwide), feeds on apples and pears, it is often called the apple maggot.

### FLASHY HIND WINGS
Underwing moths are found in Europe, Asia, and America. The Bronze underwing, *Catocala cara*, is a North American species, whose range covers Canada to Florida.

**PINES ARE FINE**
By feeding on pine trees, the caterpillar of the Resin-gall moth, *Petrova resinella* (Europe, N. America, and Asia), causes lumps of resin to be released.

**ELEPHANT, HAWK, OR MOTH?**
The attractive Elephant Hawkmoth, *Deilephila elpenor* (Europe and Asia), gets its name from the trunklike shape of the caterpillar.

*Moth can be seen at dusk hovering in front of flowers from which it feeds*

**LOOPING ALONG** *left*
The caterpillar of the Swallowtail moth, *Ourapteryx sambucaria* (Europe and Asia), moves its body by a series of "looping" actions. In the United States, similar caterpillars are called inchworms, or measuring worms.

Skull and crossbones

**SKULL-LIKE MARKINGS**
One of the most interesting moths is the Death's-head Hawkmoth, *Acherontia atropos* (Europe, Asia, and Africa). Not only does it have a skull-like pattern on its body, but it also squeaks if disturbed. The caterpillar feeds on the leaves of the potato plant. The adult sometimes steals honey from beehives (also pp. 14–15).

*Large hairy body*

**LIKE A BROKEN TWIG**
The Buff-tip, *Phalera bucephala* (Europe and Asia), manages to look exactly like a twig when it is at rest. The yellow areas on the end of its wings and around its head explain why it is so named.

*Wing pattern blends well into a tree*

**BIG IN EUROPE**
The largest European moth, the Great Peacock moth, or Viennese Emperor, *Saturnia pyri*, belongs to the same family as the giant silk moths. It can be found mostly in southern Europe and western Asia.

*Beautiful bright green color has faded after death*

**FADED BEAUTY**
The Large Emerald, *Geometra papilionaria* (Europe and Asia), has looper or inchworm caterpillars that hibernate on twigs.

**COMPARE THE HIND WINGS**
Closely related to the Bronze Underwing (opposite page), the Clifden Nonpareil, *Catocala fraxini*, is found throughout Europe and Asia. Its beautiful hind wings have a very different pattern to its duller forewings.

*Eyespots for startling predators*

*Wing span up to nearly 3 in (7 cm)*

**A DRINKING HABIT**
*Phihtdoria potatoria* is known as the Drinker because of the caterpillar's habit of drinking dew off the grasses on which it feeds. It is found in damp places throughout Europe, and in Asia as far as Japan.

*Strongly patterned hind wing*

*Beautiful reddish-brown coloring provides good camouflage when at rest*

# Exotic moths

**B**ECAUSE MOST MOTHS HIDE during the day, it is easy to forget that many of them are just as colorful and exotic-looking as butterflies. This is especially true of moths that live in the tropical and subtropical regions of Africa, Asia, Australia, and South and Central America. Here, the nights are full of the most amazing-looking moths, many of which have never been seen except by the collectors who seek them out. During the daytime, most of these moths conceal themselves in the lush tropical vegetation. At night, photography of moths in the wild is difficult, and still in its early stages. It is therefore revealing to look at the great variety of color, pattern, and shape of the tropical species shown over the next four pages.

**MOTH ROCKET**
The curious-looking "rocket-like" tufts of the Noctuid moth, *Epicausis mithii* (Madagascar), are probably scales that emit scent.

*"Rocketlike" tufts at the tip of the abdomen*

**POTATO PEST**
A destroyer of sweet potatoes, the Sweet potato Hornworm, *Agrius cinqulatus*, is found in South, Central, and North America.

*Long forewings*

**TIGER MOTH BIPLANE**
In the 1920s, the British aircraft maker Geoffrey de Havilland named an entire range of two-seater light planes after powerful-flying insects such as the Tiger moth.

*Long forewings*

**STRONG FLIER**
Like most hawkmoths, the beautiful Verdant Hawkmoth, *Euchloron megaera* (Africa), has a thick body and is a powerful flier.

*Thick body*

*Transparent wings*

**BUTTERFLY SHAPE**
The shape of its wings make this Chalcosine moth, *Agalope caudata* (Japan), look less like a moth than a butterfly.

*Feathery moth antenna*

**ABORIGINE FOOD** *above*
This Hepialid moth, *Charagia mirabilis*, comes from Australia. Hepialid caterpillars are the "witchity grubs" collected and eaten by Australian Aborigines.

**DAY-FLYING BEAUTY** *left*
Among the most attractive of the tropical moth families is the Uraniidae. This day-flying Uraniid, *Alcides aurora*, with its feathery hind wing, is found in New Guinea and the Solomon Islands.

**MOTH MIMIC**
The Pterothysanid moth, *Hibrildes norax* (Africa), flies by day and mimics a distasteful butterfly. To add to its camouflage, it even folds its wings over its back like a butterfly.

*Male with scent tufts at tip of abdomen*

**TRAILING TAILS** *below*
One of the strikingly beautiful Saturniidae family, the Madagascan Moon moth, *Argema mittrei*, has large startling eyespots on its wings.

**EAST AND WEST** *right*
In this old engraving, two South American hawkmoths, of the species *Xylopanes chiron*, are seen with an Asian moth, *Euchromia polymena* (top).

*Males usually have strongly feathered antennae*

*Thorax densely covered with hair*

*Trailing hind wing comes away if moth is attacked by predator*

**MULTICOLORED BRILLIANCE** *right*
Not surprisingly, the beautiful Jamaican Uraniid moth, *Urania sloanus*, is often mistaken for a butterfly. A closer look reveals the long, slender, moth antennae.

*Delicately fringed tail*

**FLASHY TYPE**
Like other Castniid moths, *Cyanostola hoppi* (C. America) is a day-flier with bright colors on its hind wings. When the resting moth moves, the flash of color scares away would-be predators.

*Startling color on hind wings*

*Fernlike antenna*

**SHAPE BREAKER**
When resting, this Noctuid moth from South America holds its hind wings slightly in front of its forewings. This will confuse predators by breaking up the moth's shape. The tufts or long scales are hair pencils (pp. 56–57) for the male moth to disperse its scent.

**BIG MOTH, SMALL FAMILY**
The Brahmaeidae are one of the smallest moth families, with only about 20 known species. This Brahmaeid moth, *Brahmaea wallichii*, with its wonderful swirling camouflage pattern, comes from Southeast Asia.

*Striking camouflage pattern includes startling eyespot*

*Continued on next page*

*Camouflage is improved by the clear areas on the forewings, resembling a torn leaf*

**KEEPING AN EYE OPEN**
When this Saturniid, *Ludia dentata* (Africa), moves its forewings, they reveal "eyes" that are meant to scare off predators.

*Startling eyespot*

*Distinctive long tails on hind wings distract predators*

**TRAILING WINGS**
The intricate pattern of scales and the curious wing shape of the Tailed Saturniid moth, *Copiopteryx decerto* (S. America), make this a very distinctive moth.

**ADDED PROTECTION**
The Pericopine moth, *Chetone phyleis* (S. America), mimics a distasteful *Heliconius* butterfly (pp. 56–57).

*Section resembles a torn leaf*

*Pale counter-shading of the forewing adds to the moth's camouflage when resting*

**NEWLY EMERGED MOTHS**
When it emerges from the pupa, a moth's crumpled wings give it an unreal appearance (pp. 24–25).

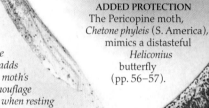

**WELL CAMOUFLAGED**
Few large moths are better at blending into the background than the Saturniid, *Loxolomia serpentina* (S. America).

**WARNING WINGS** *below*
If the West African Eupterotid moth, *Acrojan rosacea*, is disturbed, it flashes its hind wings to startle any would-be predator.

**LEAFLIKE CAMOUFLAGE**
Although little is known about the Midilid moth, *Eupastrana fenestrata* (S. America), it seems to have an effective decaying-leaf camouflage.

**NASTY TO EAT**
The Chalcosiine moth, *Campylotes kotzschi* (India), is avoided by birds, who sense from its warning colors that it is unpleasant to eat.

*Plain-colored forewings camouflage the moth while it is resting*

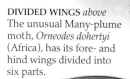

Each wing segment
fringed with scales

Long labial palp may
be for examining
food

**DIVIDED WINGS** *above*
The unusual Many-plume
moth, *Orneodes dohertyi*
(Africa), has its fore- and
hind wings divided into
six parts.

The temperate adult Emperor moth, *Saturnia pavonia*
(Europe), has the same fernlike antennae as the
related tropical Atlas
moth (below)

**CAREFUL
TASTER** *above*
The Chrysaugine, *Arbina
penkillana* (S. America), is
one of a group of
pyralid moths, which for
unknown reasons
have very long labial palps
(sense organs).

*Forewing
measures 8 in
(20 cm) from
tip to tip*

**DAY-FLIER**
The strikingly patterned
Agaristine moth,
*Longicella mollis*, is
a day-flier from
Indonesia.

*Male has fernlike
antennae for
detecting the
scent of females,
characteristic of
Saturniid moths*

*Shiny unscaled
area that
may confuse
predators by
reflecting light
like a mirror*

**FLASHY MOVER** *below*
Some species of
day-flying Zygaenid
moths (Southeast
Asia) have a metallic
sheen to their wings
that changes with
different angles of
light. This moth is
*Erasmia pulchella*.

**MONSTER MOTH**
Atlas moths, such as
this *Archaeoattacus
edwardsi* (India), are
among the largest
moths in the world;
certainly their wing area
is greater than any other
species of moth.

**MOTH OR WASP?** *below*
Because the curious
pattern and long
antennae of this
Agaristine moth,
*Cocytius durvilli* (New
Guinea), resemble a bee
or wasp in flight, it is left
alone by predators.

*Bright colors warn
predators that the
moth is distasteful
to eat*

*Transparent
wings help to
make the moth
look like a wasp*

# Day-flying moths

MOTHS ARE USUALLY THOUGHT to be creatures of the night. While this is true of the majority of the 150,000 species, there are a large number that are day-fliers. Many moths will fly by day if disturbed, but the ones illustrated on these two pages are specialized day-fliers. Flying during the day means that in many ways they behave like butterflies, but the structure of their bodies, particularly the way in which their front and hind wings link together, shows that they are moths. Many of them can be seen around flowers, and are often mistaken for butterflies. But their wing shapes are usually different and their antennae do not generally end in a club (pp. 6–7). There are, however, always exceptions: the Zygaenid moths have swollen antennae, and species of Urania moths have butterfly-shaped wings, although their antennae are slender and mothlike. Some of these insects belong to families in which the majority are night-fliers, while others, like the Zygaenidae, are mainly day-flying moths. Day-fliers include many interesting species such as the Hummingbird Hawkmoth, which hovers in front of flowers, sucking out nectar with its long proboscis. Many day-flying moths are also brightly colored and conspicuous.

These two Pyralids are (top) the Gold Spot, *Pyraustra purpuralis* (Europe and Asia), and the Small Magpie, *Eurrhypara hortulata* (Europe and Asia)

**STRIPED BODY**
The wings of this Euchromiid, *Euchromia lethe* (Africa), are not as decorative as those of some moths, but it has brightly colored bands across its body. Many moths have striped bodies. Some mimic wasps, while others are even more vividly colored. This species is sometimes found on imported bananas.

*"Furry" beelike striped abdomen*

**ROOT BORER**
The Big-root Borer, or Bee moth, *Mclittia gloriosa* (N. America), bears a striking similarity to a bee. This is even more obvious from its flight and its behavior in the field. This species feeds on the roots of squashes and gourds.

*Butterfly-shaped wings and slender antennae, together with its bright colors, make this a particularly striking moth*

**SWEET TEMPTATIONS**
To encourage butterflies and moths to come to your yard, you should grow plants that attract them with nectar and perfume. Some plants, such as species of Hebe (right), Buddleia and Aster, are particularly attractive to butterflies and moths.

**POISON EATER**
Sloan's Uraniid moth, *Urania sloanus* (Jamaica), has unusual feeding habits. The caterpillars feed on species of plant that are poisonous to most animals but not to this insect, which derives protection from the poison.

**SLOW FLIER**
This Pericopine, *Gnophaela arizonae* (N. and C. America), is a slow-flying moth often found in great numbers in meadows over 8,200 ft (2,500 m) above sea level. Its slow flight, bold pattern, and daytime activity suggest that predators avoid it because it is distasteful.

**METALLIC MOTH**
This Geometrid, *Milionia paradisea* (Papua New Guinea), has metallic colors that catch the Sun as it flies. The popular idea of a brown moth is not borne out by this species.

**PREDATORS, BEWARE!**
This colorful Syntomid, *Syntomis phegea* (Europe and Asia), is common around flowers in the warmer parts of Europe and Asia. A distasteful species, it is avoided by birds.

**REFLECTOR**
The metallic appearance of this Geometrid, *Milionia exultans* (Bismarck Archipelago), is caused by scales on the wings, which have ridges along them that catch the light.

*Dot moth caterpillar*

**VARYING PATTERNS**
The Variable Burnet, *Zygaena ephialtes* (Europe and Asia), has different forms of wing pattern, with either red or yellow spots, making this day-flying moth very popular with collectors.

**COLLECTORS' FAVOURITE**
The Provence Burnet, *Zygaena occitanica* (Europe), also has variable wing patterns and is equally popular with collectors.

*Hummingbird Hawkmoth*

*Hummingbird Hawkmoth caterpillar*

*Dot moth*

**HUMMINGBIRD?**
Most reports of "hummingbirds" around flowers in Europe or Asia stem from sightings of the Hummingbird Hawkmoth, *Macroglossum stellatarum* (Europe, Asia, and N. Africa).

Hebe salicifolia *is the species of Hebe most able to cope with cold weather conditions*

*Many species of Agaristid have similar warning patterns on their wings*

**HAWKMOTH IN ACTION**
This illustration of a Hummingbird Hawkmoth is from an original drawing by Moses Harris and was produced for a new edition of his classic 18th-century work *The Aurelian* (p. 58). On the ground is the nocturnal Dot moth, *Melanchra persicariae* (Europe and Asia).

**EXOTIC AGARISTID**
Agaristids, such as *Exsula dentatrix* (Asia), are mostly tropical moths with a few representatives in North America but none in Europe. Many are day-fliers and brightly colored, often with a basic orange and black pattern.

**WARNING PATTERNS**
A number of moths have developed the bright colors of this Pericopine, *Ephestris melaxantha* (S. America). This is probably to warn predators. Most of these moths are day-flying, although little is known of their habits.

# Migration and hibernation

BIRD MIGRATION HAS BEEN KNOWN about for hundreds if not thousands of years, but the migration of butterflies and moths is a relatively recent discovery. Unlike birds, most butterflies migrate in one direction only—from the place where they were born to a new area. There are several possible reasons for this: to avoid overpopulation; to find a new home when a temporary habitat such as agricultural land is destroyed; or to respond to the changing seasons. While birds tend to migrate at the onset of bad weather, butterflies and moths often migrate when the weather improves. For example, some species move north from North Africa and southern Europe as new plant growth becomes available for egg-laying. It may not be a direct flight—they may breed on the way.

**KEY TO WORLD MAP**

- Monarch
- Hawkmoth
- Cloudless Sulfur
- Silver-Y
- Painted Lady
- African Migrant
- Bogong

**STARTING POINTS**
The map of the world (right) shows some of the principal starting points for butterfly and moth migrations. Some species have very clearly defined routes. A good example is the Bogong moth, which travels from northern to southern Australia in such numbers that it can cause problems, as it blocks factory machinery at its resting places. Other species, such as the Painted Lady, have a variety of routes across the globe.

Millions of these butterflies can be seen in the eastern US during the migration season

**MASSES OF MONARCHS**
At the American overwintering sites of the Monarch, *Danaus plexippus* (N. and C. America) the trees are covered with these large butterflies (left).

**SOUTHERN TRAVELERS** *above*
The Cloudless Sulfur, *Phoebus sennae*, migrates in the summer to areas far north of its winter range in Mexico and the southern US. Many species migrate around the Caribbean and the southern US (below).

**MARCH OF THE MONARCHS**
The Monarch travels from Canada and the eastern seaboard across North America to its winter quarters in California and Mexico. Having survived the winter, the butterflies then fly back north.

*Monarch butterfly has a wing span of up to 4 in (10 cm)*

## SAFETY IN NUMBERS? *below*
The African Migrant butterfly, *Catopsilia florella* (Africa), often travels in huge swarms. Local migrations in large numbers may occur anywhere over Africa south of the Sahara. Cars driven through swarms sometimes overheat because their radiators get clogged with dead butterflies.

AFRICA

The Silver-Y is a moth that feeds and flies by day and night

## ADVANCING NORTHWARD
The Silver-Y moth, *Autographa gamma* (Europe, Asia, and Africa), often journeys north from Africa and southern Europe, but the details of its travels have not been studied in depth. It cannot survive the winters in northern Europe, but moths that have survived farther south breed and the next generation move northward. Some fly more directly to northern Europe, others may stop and breed on the way.

EUROPE

## CAVE-DWELLERS
The Australian Bogong moth, *Agrotis infusa*, can cover the walls of buildings in Canberra as it rests during its migration. The moths fly south to caves in the Australian Alps at around 5,000 ft (1,500 m) where they spend the hot, dry months. They move north again in the cooler fall.

AUSTRALIA

## SEASONED TRAVELER *left*
The Painted Lady, *Cynthia cardui* (Europe, Asia, America, and Africa), is one of the most widespread of all butterflies and its movements have been observed in many different areas. It is a strong flier, and individuals can travel up to 600 miles (1,000 km). In Europe, for example, it moves northward each spring (right), until the adults are killed off by cold weather. Some other species of *Cynthia* are also migratory.

European Painted Ladies can even fly over high mountains in the Alps

WORLD MAP

The Painted Lady is perhaps the world's most widespread butterfly. A map of the world (left) shows some of its one-way migration routes across Europe, Asia, and Africa.

# Hibernation

Some species of butterfly and moth survive the winter as eggs, caterpillars, or pupae; other species hibernate as adults during the winter. This means going into a period of inactivity during which the body functions slow down so much that the insect does not need to feed. The butterfly first finds a sheltered spot protected from the weather—this may be in a cave, under leaves, in a shed, or even inside a house. Hibernating butterflies are harmless and should not be disturbed during the winter.

## IN SEARCH OF SUMMER *below*
The day-flying Hummingbird Hawkmoth, *Macroglossum stellatarum* (Europe, N. Africa, and Asia), migrates from the warmer southern parts to the northern parts of Europe as the spring turns to summer and it is better able to survive.

As with all hawkmoths, this moth is a strong flier and can travel long distances easily

## EVERY HOME SHOULD HAVE ONE
Two well-known European butterflies that hibernate are the Small Tortoiseshell (right and left), *Aglais urticae*, and the Peacock, *Inachis io* (center). Both often hibernate in houses or outbuildings.

## HIBERNATING HERALD *above*
The Herald moth, *Scoliopterix libatrix* (Europe, Asia, N. Africa, and N. America), is often found hibernating in caves. As in this photograph, warm air produces beads of moisture on the wings of the insect.

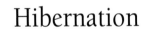
Peacock

# Shape, color, and pattern

MOTHS ARE AMONG the most colorful creatures in the world. Butterflies have been described as "flying flowers," but moths have unrivaled wing patterns, in addition to showing more variation in the shape of their wings. Color and pattern play important roles in the lives of these insects. They may provide protection by means of camouflage (pp. 50–51), or they may help to advertise a moth's presence. By making the insect conspicuous, the colors may remind predators that the creature is distasteful and should be avoided; bright colors may also be imitative of a dangerous insect such as a wasp—another way of deterring predators. On the other hand, striking colors may also help to attract a mate.

**MOTH OR WASP?**
The day-flying Hornet Clearwing moth, *Sesia apiformis* (America, Europe, and Asia), looks like a hornet and even has a similar flight pattern. Few predators would be rash enough to risk attacking this insect.

**SHARP DRESSER**
The Noctuid *Apsara radians* (Asia) has a thornlike wing pattern.

**VANISHING OUTLINE**
Markings disguise the shape of the African Noctuid *Mazuca strigicincta*.

**DISAPPEARING TRICK**
The Noctuid *Diphthera festiva* (C. and S. America) is almost invisible against a suitable background.

**DELICATE PATTERNS**
This Noctuid, *Baorisa hiero-glyphica* (E. Asia), has lines and stripes that break up its wings.

**PUTTING OFF BIRDS**
The caterpillar of the Alder moth, *Acronicta alni* (Europe), looks like a bird dropping when it is small. In its later stages, it takes on a more aggressive appearance as the white markings are replaced by orange. Hairs along its back give it its unusual shape.

*Wing pattern acts as camouflage*

False "eyes"

Flagella

**FEARSOME FOE**
The caterpillar of the Puss moth, *Cerura vinula* (Europe and Asia), uses red markings and false "eyes" in its aggression display. It also waves the threadlike extensions (flagella) on its tail.

**EYES IN THE DARK**
Shape and pattern combine to make this Sematurid moth, *Nothus lunus* (C. and S. America), inconspicuous at rest. The eyespots on the tail may be used to deter predators, although this has not yet been observed in the wild.

*Eyespot*

**PEARL OF THE ORIENT**
This Pyralid moth, *Margaronia quadrimaculalis* (E. Asia), has pearl-like white wings, broken up by a brown pattern.

**MOTH IN WASP'S CLOTHING**
This Pyralid, *Glyphodes militans* (E. Asia), gains some protection because its body looks like a wasp's.

**SPOTTED WINGS**
The forewings of the Thyridid *Rhodononeura limatula* (Madagascar) provide effective camouflage.

**BIRD DECOY**
The Uraniid moth, *Micronia astheniata* (Asia), has lines that break up its pale-colored wings. The tail spots may attract birds to peck the wings rather than the delicate body.

**CONFUSION OF COLORS**
*Cerace xanthocosma* (Japan), with its spots and swirls of color, is aptly named the Kaleidoscope moth.

**RED FOR DANGER**
The Arctiid *Composia credula* (W. Indies) has a pattern of red and black, warning predators that it is distasteful.

**THE LARGEST MOTH** *below*
Being so large presents problems of defense for the Ghost moth, *Thysania agrippina* (C. and S. America). For protection, it uses its delicate wing pattern as camouflage against tree trunks.

*Tail goes up to indicate aggression*

*Wing span up to 12 in (30 cm)*

**A CROSS LOBSTER**
The caterpillar of the Lobster moth, *Stauropus fagi* (Europe and Asia), looks like a lobster when in a defensive posture. The head goes up and back, while the tail is held up and forward. Like the Puss moth caterpillar, it also waves its tail.

**WAVY LINES**
In the Tortricid *Acleris emargana* (N. America, Europe, and Asia), the principle of camouflage is to avoid straight lines in its pattern—the forewing is particularly wavy. The forewings conceal the white hind wings at rest and the moth "vanishes" against its background.

*Wavy forewing*

**"LONG-TAILED" MOTH**
*Himantopterus marshalii*, a Zygaenid moth from Africa, is given its distinctive shape by long hind wings that look like tails. The moth flutters above the grass with the hind wings floating up and down behind.

*Distinctive hind wing is like a long tail*

# Camouflage

ALL WILD CREATURES have ways of protecting themselves from their enemies. For edible butterflies and moths, a successful way of avoiding an early death is to "disappear" into their surroundings. They may do this by mimicking another object, or they may take on the patterns and colors of local trees, rocks, or leaves. Because they are especially vulnerable in daylight hours, many caterpillars and resting moths have perfected the art of concealment. Butterflies, which are active by day and which usually rest with their wings together over their backs, have adopted other forms of camouflage. Some forest butterflies rest like moths, with their wings spread out, while other species disguise themselves as either living or decaying leaves. The butterfly that has perfected this clever form of camouflage is the Indian Leaf butterfly— it is truly a master of disguise.

**DEADLY ENEMY** *left*
One of the main reasons why many moths and butterflies camouflage themselves is to escape from predatory birds.

*Butterfly's upright head*

*Butterfly's wing*

Leaf butterfly at rest on stem

Brown underside of Leaf butterfly

Orange-and-blue top side of Leaf butterfly

**INDIAN LEAF-TRICK**
The most dramatic example of butterfly camouflage is the Indian Leaf butterfly, *Kallima inachus* (S. E. Asia). At rest, the butterfly bears a remarkably close resemblance to a decaying leaf on a stem. It frequently rests on the ground in leaf litter, where it becomes virtually invisible.

*Resemblance to stalk and veins of a leaf*

54

**WRONG PECKING ORDER** *left*
The tiny spots on the tail of this Uraniid moth, *Cyphura pardata* (New Guinea), may well distract birds, which might otherwise peck at more vital parts of its body. The moth can then escape, even if its wing is slightly torn. The main part of the wings shows a disruptive pattern when the insect is at rest.

**CITY MOTH, COUNTRY MOTH** *right*
Some years ago, it was realized that the city form of the Peppered moth, *Biston betularia* (Europe), had gradually changed from a light to a black color. This was to escape birds, which could easily spot a light-colored moth on a smoke-polluted tree. In the countryside, the same moth is still speckled white.

*Disruptive wing pattern*

Black form

Speckled form

**NOT LIKE A MOTH** *right*
These Noctuid moths, photographed in a Costa Rican rainforest, are completely protected by their uncanny resemblance to lichen on lichen-covered bark.

**DISAPPEARING CATERPILLAR** *left*
By blending with the bark of a tree, this Lappet moth caterpillar (species unknown) is completely protected from predators during daylight hours.

**DECAYING LEAF** *above*
This South American Leaf moth, *Belenoptera sanguine*, reproduces a "dead-leaf" pattern on its wings, including the "skeletonized" part often found on dead leaves. When resting, the moth rolls the front part of its wings to resemble a leaf stalk.

Peppered moth resting on tree in Sherwood Forest, England

*Clear areas that give impression of torn leaf*

**DAMAGED LEAF** *above*
To make its leaf camouflage more realistic, this green Pyralid moth, *Siga liris* (S. America), has irregularly shaped clear areas in its wings. When the moth is resting, these give the impression of a damaged leaf.

Notodontid moth (S. America)

*Woodlike camouflage*

Notodontid moth (S. America)

**WOOD BORER** *above*
The caterpillar of this Carpenter moth (C. America) bores into trees. As an adult, the moth is almost invisible against bark (right).

**SPOT THE MOTH** *above*
It would be impossible to find a better example of how well a moth can blend in with its surroundings than this beautifully patterned but unknown species of carpenter moth.

**VANISHING MOTHS**
These three pinned moths have been left with their wings in a normal resting position to show how succesful their camouflage is. In order to survive, they must not look like moths or they would soon be detected by a hungry bird or lizard.

Saturniid moth, *Automeris* species (S. America)

*Dead-leaf camouflage*

# Mimicry and other unusual behavior

ALTHOUGH MOST BUTTERFLIES and moths live "normal" lives, there are species that behave unusually. They include moths that can swim underwater, and others whose caterpillars live in ants' nests or beehives. There is also the amazing way in which some species of Lepidoptera mimic other species. If some tropical butterflies seem to advertise themselves with their garish colors and slow flight, it is usually because they are poisonous to predators. But don't be fooled by the "same species" of butterfly flying nearby; it is not poisonous at all, just a very good mimic.

Fruit with hole where adult moth (above right) has pushed its way out after pupation

*Caterpillar*

**JUMPING BEAN MOTH**
Jumping Beans, or "pocket pets," are not beans at all, but the caterpillar of *Cydia saltitans* (C. America). The "bean" is a small fruit that the caterpillar has bored its way into. When placed near heat, the caterpillar twists and jumps. This may be to move the fruit, with the caterpillar inside, out of direct sunlight.

Mimic Dismorphiine butterfly, *Dismorphia orise*, Family Pieridae

Distasteful Ithomoiine butterfly, *Methona confusa*, Family Nymphalidae

**SUGAR CANE PEST**
The caterpillars of this Galleriid moth, *Eldana saacharina*, are a menace in Africa because they bore into sugar cane stems.

**DANGEROUS TO CATTLE**
This Pyraustine moth, *Filodes sexpunctalis*, is a species of moth that uses its proboscis to feed on the liquid around the eyes of cattle. In doing so it transmits diseases.

**FLOATING MOTH**
The caterpillar of this Brown China-mark moth, *Elophila nympheata* (Europe and Asia), lives in waterplants (see opposite page).

**AN ENEMY IN THE HIVE**
Beekeepers have to watch for the caterpillars of the Wax moth, *Galleria* (N. America). The caterpillar not only feeds on the wax, but also destroys the honeycomb by making silk-lined galleries (right).

Mimic Danaid butterfly, *Lycorea phenarete*, Family Nymphalidae

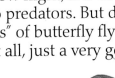

Noctuid moth (species and place of origin unknown)

*Scent tuft has been artificially turned outward*

Arctiid moth, *Creatonotos gangis* (Australia and Asia)

Mimic Castniid moth, *Gazera linus*, Family Castniidae

**USING THE RIGHT SCENT**
The strange-looking tufts protruding from both these moths' abdomens are known as hair pencils. Evident only in certain species of butterfly and moth, the tufts are a way for the male to disperse his scent and attract a female during courtship.

**COPYING YOUR NEIGHBOR**
Although these four South American "butterflies" look amazingly alike, not only do they all belong to different families, but one of them is also in fact a moth. The moth and two of the butterflies are protected because the Ithomiine butterfly they mimic is distasteful to predators (more on mimicry on the opposite page).

*Transparent wing covered with fine hairs but few scales*

*Scales*

**A WATERPLANT SHELTER**
This is the adult Brown China-mark moth (see opposite page) and its caterpillar, after the larva has built a shelter in a waterplant.

**SILVER FLASH**
The Silver butterfly, *Argyrophorus argenteus,* is one of the most spectacular South American butterflies. As it flies in the high mountain areas of the Andes, its silvery metallic wings reflect the light, making the butterfly seem to appear and disappear.

**GHOST OF THE RAINFOREST**
The Clearwing butterfly, *Haetera macleannania,* lives in the jungles of South and Central America, where its ghostlike appearance make it almost invisible. Butterflies and moths with transparent wings have fewer scales than other Lepidoptera.

*Caterpillar in leafy shelter on underside of waterplant*

**SEASONAL SWITCH** *below and below left*
Although the two butterflies on the left look very different, they are in fact both Pansy butterflies, *Precis octavia* (Africa). The Pansy has a different pattern if it develops in the wet rather than the dry season.

*Dry Season form*

*Wing coupling mechanism like that of moths*

**THE OLDEST AUSTRALIAN?** *above*
Because it is the only butterfly with a wing mechanism like a moth's, the Australian Regent Skipper butterfly, *Euschemon rafflesia,* may be one of the world's most primitive butterflies.

**A BAD-TEMPERED BABY** *below*
It may look sweet, but the Saddleback caterpillar of this tropical Limacodid moth is best left alone; the hairs on its spines are poisonous to the touch.

**PRIZE MIMICS** *below*
In this mimicry chain, the Ecuador Small Postman butterfly mimics his equally poisonous rainforest neighbor, the Ecuador Postman butterfly. The two Brazilian subspecies (right) look even more alike.

*Wet Season form*

# Mimicry

One of the most dramatic ways that certain species of butterflies and moths protect themselves is by mimicking neighboring species of Lepidoptera. This often takes the form of an edible species copying the color pattern of a species with an unpleasant smell or taste. Birds and other predators learn to recognize the warning patterns or bright colors of the harmful species and leave it alone—a form of protection that extends to the mimic species that is edible.

Small Postman butterfly, *Heliconius erato* (Ecuador)

Postman butterfly, *Heliconius melpomene* (Ecuador)

Small Postman butterfly, *Heliconius erato* (Brazil)

Postman butterfly, *Heliconius melpomene* (Brazil)

# Endangered species

*Painted eyespot*

**D**EPENDENT AS THEY ARE ON WILD PLANTS and open countryside, butterflies and moths are especially vulnerable to changes in the environment, especially those caused by human beings. In recent times many of these beautiful insects have become first rare, then endangered, then extinct. Butterflies and moths are more common in the tropics than in Europe or North America, but even there the destruction of the rainforest has reduced their numbers and variety. In milder climates, people's need for land has resulted in the loss of habitats, and many insects have become endangered. Many of these species are listed in the Red Data Book of the International Union for the Conservation of Nature.

**BUTTERFLY FRAUD** *above*
This famous butterfly fraud dates from about 1702. After painting eyespots on the wings of Brimstone butterflies, the "collector" claimed they were a new species of butterfly, later described as *"Papilio ecclipsis"*

*Badly torn wing*

**EARLY COLLECTOR** *below*
Our knowledge of Lepidoptera is based largely on the work of early collectors such as the Englishman Moses Harris, whose classic book *The Aurelian* was published in 1766.

*Large wings and long tails typical of swallowtails*

**UNDER THREAT**
The Philippines Swallowtail butterfly, *Papilio chikae*, was discovered in the 1960s. Not only is its habitat threatened, but it is also in danger from illegal collection.

**LONG-TAILED BEAUTY**
Surely the most beautiful European moth, the Spanish Moon moth, *Graellsia isabellae* (French Alps and Central Spain), now has to be protected by law.

*The only European Saturniid moth with tails on its hind wings*

Old engraving of pinned butterfly

## Innocent casualties

"As dead as a dodo" is the sad phrase we use for a creature that has become extinct. In the United States, the Xerces Blue butterfly has vanished; in Britain, several once-common species are now extinct. In Britain, enthusiasts have tried to introduce related subspecies from the European mainland to replace the vanished British species. But in other parts of the world extinct species cannot be replaced; and many beautiful insects are now just as dead as the dodo.

The Essex Emerald moth, *Thetidia smaragdaria* (Europe), is now extinct in Britain

Engraving of 19th-century collecting box (left)

*Once found in coastal sand dunes of California*

**IN MEMORY OF**
The Xerces Society, a worldwide conservation group, was formed in memory of the California Xerces Blue, *Glauscopsyche xerces*, last seen near San Francisco in 1941.

**MAKING A COMEBACK** *left*
After their habitats were largely destroyed, the Large Copper and the Large Blue became extinct in Britain. Now, subspecies of both butterflies have been introduced from the European mainland into specially chosen areas of England.

The Large Blue butterfly, *Maculinea arion* (Europe), was recently reintroduced into southwest England

The beautiful Large Copper butterfly, *Lycaena dispar* (Europe), became extinct in Britain in the 1800s (p. 28)

*Very large, beautifully marked wings*

**THE DISAPPEARING AMERICAN**
The Regal Fritillary butterfly, *Speyeria idalia,* occurs in Canada and a number of American States. But as its natural grassland habitat is plowed up, the butterfly has become increasingly rare.

**19TH-CENTURY COLLECTOR**
The Musée Nationale d'Histoire Naturelle, Paris; the Smithsonian, Washington; the Natural History Museum, London; and other great national collections, were all built up by dedicated collections.

**NO FOREST, NO BUTTERFLIES** *above*
A far greater threat to butterflies and moths than collectors or disease has been the increasing destruction of their habitats. Many countries now have laws preventing excessive collecting, and so fewer species have been destroyed by collectors. But throughout the world, important habitats, like this Central American rainforest, are being lost to new farmlands and towns. Many harmless insects are also killed by herbicides and insecticides.

**MOUNTAIN RARITY** *left*
The Corsican Swallowtail butterfly, *Papilio hospiton,* is found only in the mountainous regions of Corsica and Sardinia. Never numerous, its collection is now forbidden by law.

*This specimen is of the more colorful male; females can have wing spans of 11 in (28 cm)*

**COLLECTORS' FAVORITE** *below*
Found only in Jamaica, the large Homerus Swallowtail butterfly, *Papilio homerus,* is unfortunately popular with collectors. It is now on the list of endangered species (also pp. 26–27).

**BEAUTIFUL BIRDWING**
One of the largest known butterflies, the Queen Alexandra's Birdwing, *Ornithoptrea alexandrae* (New Guinea), has suffered from the destruction of its forest habitat and the activities of collectors.

**NO LONGER A PEST** *below*
Increasingly scarce in mainland Europe, the Black-veined White butterfly, *Aporia crataegi,* is already extinct in Britain. Its caterpillars used to be a pest of fruit trees.

*Easily recognizable large wings and long tails of many swallowtails*

*Characteristic contrasting light and dark colors of most swallowtails*

**HERE TODAY, GONE TOMORROW?**
Although the Zebra Swallowtail, *Eurytides marcellinus,* can be found in several parts of Canada and the United States, it is threatened by the destruction of its food plant, as well as by suburban growth.

# Watching butterflies and moths

F OR MANY YEARS, people have collected butterflies and moths as a hobby and for scientific study. But it is better for the insects themselves, as well as more interesting and rewarding, to watch them in the field. You can also photograph butterflies, or catch them in a net for closer examination before releasing them again. Most moths fly at night, but it is possible to study members of day-flying families. When watching butterflies and moths, you can discover the answers to many questions about their behavior. Do they feed at a certain time of day? Do they have a territory, and if so, how do they defend it? Do they migrate, and if so, when? Do their flight patterns change in different seasons? Studying butterflies in this way is simple: you do not require much equipment, and you won't need to harm them—all you need is patience.

A 19th-century interpretation of the fashion for insect collecting

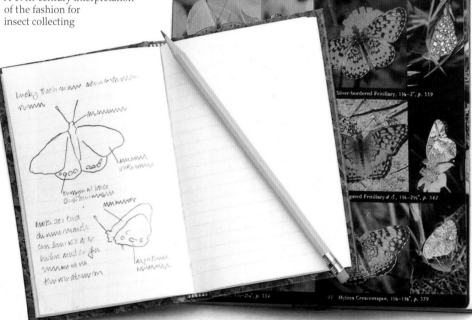

**PINNING THEM DOWN**
Compiling a butterfly collection was once a popular pastime.

**WARNING FOR COLLECTORS**
Many butterflies are protected by law, and in some countries collecting without a permit is forbidden. Collecting and study on nature reserves is usually also carefully controlled. A number of butterflies cannot be collected and sent out of the country without a permit. International conventions regulate trade in endangered species. Always check local regulations.

**WRITING AND RECORDING**
Use a notebook (above) or voice recorder (below) to make notes on each butterfly's appearance and behavior, together with the date, time, weather conditions, and details of the locality. A good field guide helps in identification.

**CLOSE-UP CAMERA**
A digital camera with built-in or snap-on macro lens, which allows extreme close-ups of small subjects, is ideal. Bright sunlight will give the best results; use flash in the shade.

*Some compact cameras can be used for "macro" close-ups*

**SHORT-FOCUS TELESCOPE**
In the field, use an 8 x 20 short-focus optical telescope (which has a magnification of x 8 and a lens diameter of 20 mm).

## PILL BOXES

Glass or plastic lids allow you to examine an insect and later to release it unharmed. Do not keep specimens in pill boxes for too long.

*Pill boxes*

## IN FULL PURSUIT

This 19th-century collector is using a large clap-net, a type of net formerly used for catching birds. In the 1800s, people saw insect collecting as a harmless hobby.

## USING THE NET

Sweep the net through the air in the direction shown below. As you double the net back, the butterfly will be directed toward the bottom. A final rapid flick of the wrist traps the insect in the net. When using the net in this way, be careful to avoid thorns and sharp twigs that may damage both the mesh and the insect.

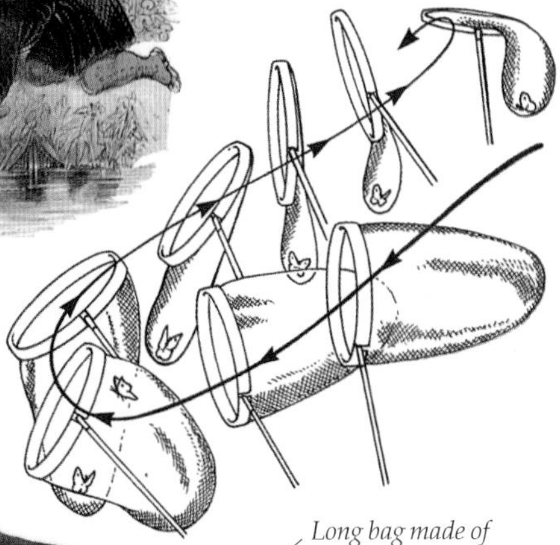

*Collecting jar*

## COLLECTING JARS

Insert a twig for the insect to perch on in each jar. The specimen will then keep still and not damage itself by fluttering around.

## CLOSE-UP VIEW

Examination under an eyeglass is often the only way to see specialized features mentioned in books.

All-purpose sweep net for collecting insects—not suitable for butterflies

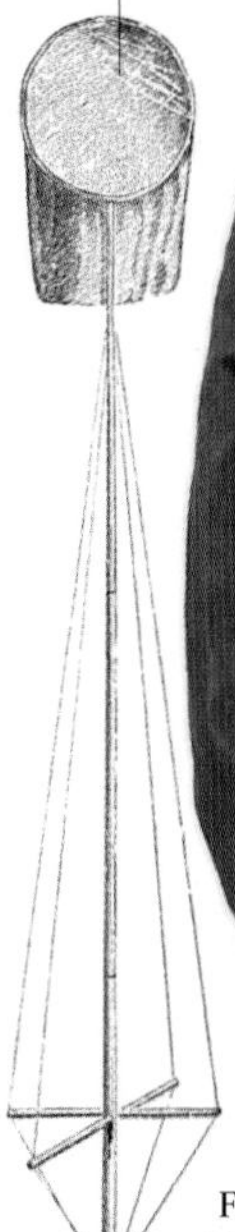

*Emperor net*

*Rounded end of bag reduces risk of damaging butterfly*

*Long bag made of fine material to protect butterfly; dark mesh is less conspicuous than lighter fabric*

## FOR HIGH-FLIERS

The emperor net was devised to catch butterflies that lived in the treetops, such as the Purple Emperor, *Apatura iris* (Europe and Asia; p. 29).

# Raising butterflies and moths

An elaborate 19th-century "caterpillar house"

Many butterflies and moths are easy to raise from egg to adult, provided that the basic conditions are right. You should always handle the insects with care, keep the temperature close to that of the natural habitat, and give each species its own specific food plant. In addition, food for caterpillars must be fresh—either in the form of freshly plucked leaves or complete, pot-grown plants. Sometimes, the food may appear to be in good condition but the caterpillars will not eat it. The reason is usually the state of the plant—if it is short of water, or if it is too old, the caterpillars may reject it. We still know little about the exact needs of plant-feeding caterpillars: although some are choosy about their food, other species, such as some of the Pyralid moths, whose caterpillars feed on grain or flour, are easy to raise. Adult butterflies and moths, if they take any food at all, will sometimes feed from cut flowers or the flowers of potted plants. Many will sip happily at a weak solution of sugar or honey in water. But in general you should not keep adults in captivity for long. Once they have emerged, release them when weather conditions are right.

## Keeping caterpillars

Keep caterpillars in a special cage, or in a muslin sleeve over the food plant itself. Although many species take food from only one plant, some caterpillars will eat a wide variety of food. Given the opportunity, there are caterpillars who will even eat objects they cannot survive on such as plastics and artificial fibers.

*Mesh covering*

*Wooden frame*

**FINE MESH CAGE**
The soft walls of a fine mesh caterpillar cage protect its delicate inhabitants. A zipper gives you access to the contents; paper catches any debris.

*Food plant*

*Newspaper*

*Plastic tray acts as cage base*

**HANDLE WITH CARE**
Caterpillars are very delicate. The safest way to pick them up is with a fine paintbrush. Some larvae have stinging hairs—another reason for handling them in this way.

**HOMEGROWN FOOD**
Foods grown in the cage itself will be attractive to most caterpillars, but the larvae eat so much you should keep extra plants in reserve.

**PLANT-POT CAGE**
You can attach a sleeve of muslin to a small pot and raise caterpillars on a growing plant. Make sure that the caterpillars do not strip the leaves and kill the plant.

*Newspaper*

*Zipper for opening*

## RAISING OAK SILK MOTHS
Here the caterpillars of the Oak Silk moth, *Antheraea harti* (Asia), are being raiseed on cut oak twigs that are kept fresh in water. Although the leaves stay fresh for some time, more food will soon be needed. It is best to keep the insects and their food in a cage, even though these caterpillars are usually so busy eating that they will only move from leaf to leaf.

*Silk moth caterpillars eating oak leaves*

*Oak silk moth cocoon*

*Oak silk moth cocoon*

*Paper plug protects caterpillars from the risk of drowning*

*Water*

*Twigs touch tabletop so that caterpillars can climb back up if they fall off*

# Keeping adults
When the adult insects have emerged from their pupae, they will require a different food source. Either a selection of cut flowers or a weak solution of honey and water can be used. Alternatively, you can provide fruit juice (see below). Butterflies may mate before you release them, providing eggs so that you can start the life cycle over again.

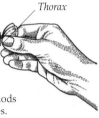
*Thorax*

## HANDLING BUTTERFLIES
Hold the butterfly gently at the base of the wings, making sure not to squeeze the thorax. Pressure on the thorax will harm the insect and is one of the methods collectors use to kill butterflies.

## MOVING MOTHS
You can sometimes persuade a moth to move onto one of your fingers. You can then transfer it to a cage for breeding or study.

*Thorax*

Cracker butterfly, *Hamadryas feronia* (N., C., and S. America)

*Proboscis*

## FRUIT-JUICE FEEDERS
Give butterflies and moths pieces of fruit so that they can feed on the juice. This is a technique widely used in butterfly houses, where a wide variety of fruit may be used.

## "THE BUTTERFLIES' HAUNT"
This 19th-century painting by W. Scott Myles shows the corner of a meadow with species of European butterflies congregating around favorite food plants such as dandelions, thistles, and various grasses. By growing the right types of flowers and grasses, you can attract butterflies to your yard.

# Butterfly classification

With ABOUT 170,000 known species, butterflies and moths make up one of the largest groups of insect. More kinds are discovered every year. To make sense of this huge diversity, lepidopterists (scientists who study butterflies and moths) classify species by giving them unique two-part scientific names. These names work like identity tags and are recognized by specialists all over the world. Species are organized into groups of increasing size, and the characteristics they share help to show how different kinds of butterflies and moths have evolved.

*Antennae with expanded tips*

White Admiral, *Ladoga camilla*

*Short, brush-tipped front legs*

**Order** Lepidoptera
**Superfamily** Papilionoidea
**Family** Nymphalidae
**Genus** *Danaus*
**Species** *plexippus*

## CLASSIFICATION LEVELS
Like all living things, the Monarch butterfly has its own two-part scientific name. It is classified as the species *Danaus plexippus*, which belongs to the genus *Danaus*, and the family Nymphalidae. This family, in turn, belongs to the superfamily Papilionoidea—one of several dozen superfamilies in the order Lepidoptera, which includes all the world's butterflies and moths.

## CLASSIFYING BUTTERFLIES AND MOTHS
When a butterfly or moth is classified, scientists examine the features that it shares with others in its family group. White admirals, for example, have a small pair of front legs—a feature found in butterflies belonging to the family Nymphalidae. The pattern on the wings is also a key feature, as is the presence of a wing coupling device, known as a frenulum, present in most moths. Species can also be classified by studying their DNA—the substance that passes on inherited features in all living things.

## BUTTERFLY AND MOTH EVOLUTION
The family tree, or cladogram, below shows how some of the major superfamilies of butterflies and moths are linked by evolution. The most primitive lepidopterans were small insects with scale-covered wings, but without tongues that coil up. Gradually, they evolved into the enormous array of species that are alive today. Butterflies make up just two superfamilies—all the others consist of moths.

LEPIDOPTERA

| Numerous superfamilies | Gelechioidea | Tineoidea | Zygaenoidea | Sesioidea | Tortricoidea | Pterophoroidea |
|---|---|---|---|---|---|---|

| PRIMITIVE MOTHS | CASE-BEARERS AND RELATIVES | CLOTHES MOTHS AND RELATIVES | BURNET MOTHS AND RELATIVES | CLEARWING MOTHS AND RELATIVES | TORTRICID MOTHS AND RELATIVES | PLUME MOTHS AND RELATIVES |
|---|---|---|---|---|---|---|
| *Micropterix* | *Coleophora* | *Tineola bisselliella* | *Arniocera erythropyga* | *Albuna oberthuri* | *Acleris emargana* | *Pterophorus pentadactyl* |

## PAPILIONOIDEA

Black-veined White,
*Aporia crataegi*

### Family: PIERIDAE Whites and sulphurs

1,000 species

This large family of butterflies includes some important agricultural pests, also some of the world's most widespread species, such as the Large White (*Pieris brassicae*) and the Small White (*Pieris rapae*). Most of the species in the family are white, yellow, or orange.

Duke of Burgundy,
*Hamearis lucina*

### Family: RIODINIDAE Metalmark butterflies

1,000 species

Most common in the tropics, metalmarks are named after the bright metallic spots that many species have on their wings.

## HESPEROIDEA

### Family: HESPERIIDAE Skippers

3,500 species

Skippers are typically small, with wide heads and well separated antennae, which often have curved tips. They move with a rapid darting flight.

Large Skipper,
*Ochlodes venatas*

Eastern Tiger Swallowtail,
*Papilio glaucus*

### Family: PAPILIONOIDEA Swallowtails

550 species

Named after the long hind-wing tails found in many species, the swallowtail family includes the world's largest and most eye-catching butterflies. Most of its species have thickset bodies, widely spreading wings, and a mixture of flapping and gliding flight.

### Family: NYMPHALIDAE Fritillaries, admirals and monarchs

5,000 species

This large family includes many of the world's most colorful butterflies. Both sexes have reduced front legs, with brushlike tips in males. Instead of walking on six legs, nymphalids walk on four.

Red Admiral,
*Vanessa atalanta*

Adonis Blue,
*Polyommatus bellargus*

### Family: LYCAENIDAE Blues, hairstreaks, and coppers

5,000 species

Mostly small, with wingspans of 2 in (5 cm) or less, these butterflies have a fast but jerky flight. Males and females usually differ, and their wings often have a metallic sheen.

| Pyraloidea | Bombycoidea | Lasiocampoidea | Hesperoidea | Papilionoidea | Geometroidea | Noctuoidea |

**PYRALID MOTHS AND RELATIVES**
*Glyphodes militans*

**SILK MOTHS AND RELATIVES**
*Archaeoattacus edwardsi*

**LAPPET MOTHS AND RELATIVES**
*Gastropacha quercifolia*

**SKIPPER BUTTERFLIES**
*Phocides polybius*

**TYPICAL BUTTERFLIES**
*Papilio machaon*

**LOOPER MOTHS AND RELATIVES**
*Abraxas grossulariata*

**NOCTUID MOTHS AND RELATIVES**
*Scoliopteryx libatrix*

# Moth classification

LIKE BUTTERFLIES, moths are classified into family groups. The smallest contains a handful of species, but the largest—the noctuids—contains more species than all the world's butterflies combined. Within each family, species share features, such as the structure of mouthparts and wings. Here, 12 of the most important families of moth, from six different superfamilies, have been depicted. Many more families are recognized by specialists. Some consist entirely of micromoths—minute species that are hard to see with the naked eye.

## TINEOIDAE

Clothes moth,
*Tineola bisselliella*

Family: TINEIDAE Clothes moths and relatives

3,000 species

Most moths in this family are small, dusty-looking insects, with a gold or silvery sheen. Their wings are slender, and at rest, they are held over the body in an inverted "V". Their caterpillars have wide-ranging diets. Some feed on fungi or lichens, while others specialize in eating feathers, hair, or wool.

## ZYGAENOIDEA

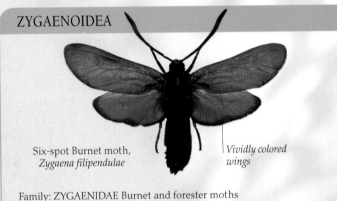

Six-spot Burnet moth,
*Zygaena filipendulae*

*Vividly colored wings*

Family: ZYGAENIDAE Burnet and forester moths

1,000 species

Burnet and forester moths are small- or medium-sized insects with brightly colored wings. They typically fly by day. Their caterpillars are stout, elongated, or slug-shaped, and often have warning colors showing that they are poisonous, like the adults.

## SESIOIDEA

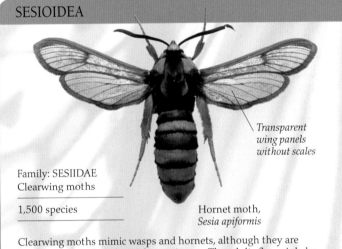

Family: SESIIDAE
Clearwing moths

1,500 species

*Transparent wing panels without scales*

Hornet moth,
*Sesia apiformis*

Clearwing moths mimic wasps and hornets, although they are harmless, since they do not have stingers. The adults fly mainly by day, and sometimes make a buzzing sound as they visit flowers.

## GEOMETROIDEA

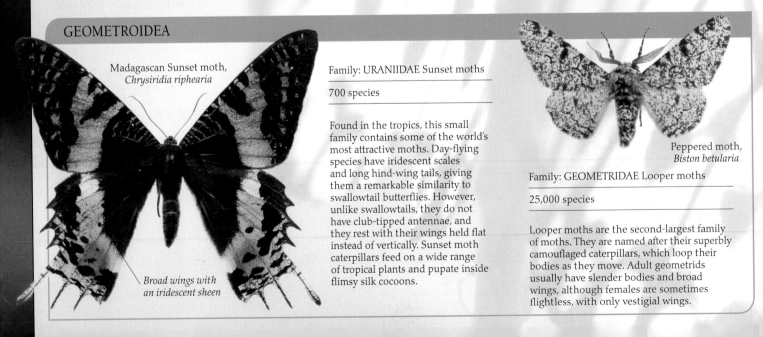

Madagascan Sunset moth,
*Chrysiridia riphearia*

Family: URANIIDAE Sunset moths

700 species

Found in the tropics, this small family contains some of the world's most attractive moths. Day-flying species have iridescent scales and long hind-wing tails, giving them a remarkable similarity to swallowtail butterflies. However, unlike swallowtails, they do not have club-tipped antennae, and they rest with their wings held flat instead of vertically. Sunset moth caterpillars feed on a wide range of tropical plants and pupate inside flimsy silk cocoons.

*Broad wings with an iridescent sheen*

Peppered moth,
*Biston betularia*

Family: GEOMETRIDAE Looper moths

25,000 species

Looper moths are the second-largest family of moths. They are named after their superbly camouflaged caterpillars, which loop their bodies as they move. Adult geometrids usually have slender bodies and broad wings, although females are sometimes flightless, with only vestigial wings.

## BOMBYCOIDEA

### Silk moth,
*Bombyx mori*

**Family: BOMBYCIDAE Silk moths**

300 species

This small family contains the domesticated silk moth, together with its close relatives. They are heavy-bodied insects. The short-lived adults do not eat and have nonfunctioning mouthparts. Silk moth caterpillars, or silkworms, have a single fleshy horn near the end of the abdomen.

### Great Peacock moth,
*Saturnia pyri*

**Family: SATURNIIDAE Saturniid moths**

1,000 species

This family of moths includes many of the world's largest species and has a distribution that stretches worldwide. The majority are brown or yellowish green, with eyespots on the wings. Adults often do not feed.

### Verdant Sphinx,
*Euchloron megaera*

**Family: SPHINGIDAE Hawkmoths**

1,200 species

Found worldwide, hawkmoths are distinctive insects with robust bodies and streamlined wings. They fly powerfully, sometimes migrating long distances to breed. They feed on nectar by using their long tongues to reach their food.

## NOCTUOIDEA

### Ilia Underwing,
*Catocala ilia*

### Gypsy moth,
*Lymantria dispar*

**Family: NOCTUIIDAE Noctuid moths**

35,000 species

The noctuid family makes up the largest group of lepidopterans. Generally broad-bodied with robust wings, they are usually drably colored in browns, yellows, and grays, although some have brightly colored underwings that help to scare predators away. They are almost entirely nocturnal, and their caterpillars include many agricultural pests.

**Family: NOTODONTIDAE Prominents**

3,500 species

These moths have a tuft of projecting scales on the hind edge of each forewing. When the wings are closed, the scales project in two prominent humps. Typically small- to medium-sized, prominents mimic lichens, bark, or broken twigs. Their caterpillars have a wide variety of shapes and include species with protective hairs or whiplike tails.

**Family: LYMANTRIDAE Tussock moths**

2,500 species

Generally medium-sized with hairy bodies, tussock moths are usually unobtrusively colored and are active at night. In many species, the caterpillars have defensive hairs grouped in tufts. Adults lack functional mouthparts and do not feed.

### Buff-tip,
*Phalera bucephala*

*Distinctive scalloped forewing margins*

**Family: ARCTIIDAE Tiger moths**

10,000 species

Tiger moths get their name from their bright patterns, which advertise the fact that they are poisonous. Plump and hairy, with broad wings, they include day-flying and nocturnal species. In some, the caterpillars are stout and thickly haired, which gives them their name "fuzzy bears". They pupate above or near ground level, inside flimsy cocoons.

*Bright markings on wings*

### Garden Tiger,
*Arctia caja*

# Butterfly and moth records

**B**UTTERFLIES AND MOTHS include some of the most beautiful and bizarre animals in the insect world. They come in a range of sizes and include some of the greatest travelers. Some of their caterpillars have astonishing diets. Others are harvested as food, but a few can prove fatal.

## LARGEST BUTTERFLY

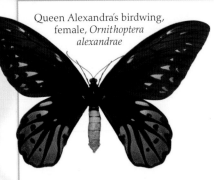

Queen Alexandra's birdwing, female, *Ornithoptera alexandrae*

Restricted to New Guinea's tropical rainforest, Queen Alexandra's birdwing is the world's largest butterfly. Females have a wingspan of up to 11 in (28 cm), while males are smaller and also more brightly colored. Once widely trapped by butterfly collectors, this species is officially listed as endangered.

## LARGEST MOTH

Atlas moth, *Attacus atlas*

Female Atlas moths have the largest wing area of any moth, measuring over 62 sq in (400 sq cm). Atlas moths live in tropical forests in South and Southeast Asia, and their caterpillars grow up on trees. Like other Saturniid moths, the adults do not feed.

## SMALLEST BUTTERFLIES

Blue butterflies from the genus *Brephidium* hold the record for the smallest wingspan in the world. Several species, including dwarf and pygmy blues, measure just ½ in (1.2 cm) between their wingtips, which is less than a common housefly.

Western Pygmy Blue, *Brephidium exilis*

## SMALLEST MOTHS

The smallest moths are far tinier than the smallest butterflies. Known as micromoths, some have wingspans as little as ⅛ in (3 mm), making them very difficult to spot. Many of these moths start life as caterpillars inside leaves. Called leaf-miners, they leave winding trails as they feed.

## LARGEST CATERPILLAR

Caterpillars of the North American Regal moth (*Citheronia regalis*) can grow up to 6 in (15 cm) long. They are known as hickory horned devils, from their food plants and impressive but harmless spines. Several kinds of hawkmoth caterpillar rival them in size.

## LONGEST ANTENNAE

Fairy Longhorn moth, *Nemophora degeerella*

Relative to their bodies, fairy longhorn moths have some of the largest antennae in the insect world, measuring up to 3–4 times their body length in males. These moths live in damp wooded habitats, and clouds of them can sometimes be seen fluttering close to tsrees.

## FASTEST MOTH

With their powerful bodies and streamlined wings, hawkmoths are among the fastest insects. Large species, such as the Death's head Hawkmoth, can reach speeds of 30 mph (50 kph). Hawkmoths are also skilled at hovering, and hang in the air as they drink nectar from flowers.

Death's head Hawkmoth, *Acherontia atropos*

## MOST DANGEROUS CATERPILLARS

Lonomia moth caterpillars from South America have highly toxic hairs. Contact with a person's bare skin can cause the person to bleed internally and sometimes even die. The hairs protect the caterpillars from most predators, although some birds are immune to them and eat the caterpillars without being harmed.

## MOST DAMAGING

Many caterpillars eat crops. Among the most damaging are the caterpillars of the Large White butterfly, which feed on cabbages and related plants, and Codling moth caterpillars, which bore into apples.

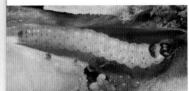

Large White, *Pieris brassicae*

Codling moth caterpillar, *Cydia pomonella*

## MOST HARVESTED CATERPILLARS

In southern Africa, caterpillars called mopane worms are widely collected as food. The caterpillars are produced by the Mopane Emperor moth (*Gonimbrasia belina*), which lays its eggs on shrubs and trees. Mopane worms are full of protein, and can be eaten cooked or raw.

## STRANGEST DIET

Horn moth caterpillars (*Ceratophaga sp.*) eat the hooves and horns of dead animals, and even the outer layer of tortoise shells. They belong to the same family as Clothes moths, and share their ability to digest keratin. Keratin is the tough protein that gives hair, hooves, and horn their strength.

## NOISIEST BUTTERFLY

Cracker butterfly, *Hamadryas arethusa*

Butterflies usually fly silently, but male cracker butterflies make a clicking sound with their wings. These sounds are probably used to ward off predators, to attract females, or to deter rival males. The clicks are made by specially thickened veins on the butterflies' forewings. Cracker butterflies live in Central and South America.

## GREATEST TRAVELERS

Every year, Monarch butterflies travel up to 3,000 miles (4,800 km) on their annual migrations across North America. They set out from their winter quarters in California and Mexico, reaching as far north as Canada. One or two generations later, the butterflies complete the return journey, before the winter cold sets in.

Monarch butterfly, *Danaus plexippus*

## MOST WIDESPREAD BUTTERFLY

The painted lady (*Vanessa cardui*) is one of the world's most successful butterflies, with an almost global range. Present year-round in warm parts of the world, it migrates to cooler regions in huge numbers, laying its eggs on a wide range of plants.

## LONGEST LIVED

Aside from hibernating species, many butterflies and moths survive for only a few weeks once they are adult. At the other extreme, some tropical butterflies—such as heliconiids—can survive for over 6 months, while fruit-eating species may live for nearly a year.

Male *Heliconius ricini*

# Glossary

*Antenna with club-shaped tips*

Monarch butterfly,
*Danaus plexippus*

**ABDOMEN** The rear part of an insect's body that has organs for reproduction and for digesting food. In caterpillars, the abdomen has two rows of prolegs, which look like fleshy stumps.

**ANTENNA** (*plural* **ANTENNAE**) Paired sensory organs on an insect's head, also known as "feelers." Antennae enable butterflies and moths to smell airborne scents, so that they can track down partners or food plants.

**BIRDWINGS** The world's largest butterflies, from southern Asia and Australia. Birdwings are related to swallowtails, but their wings do not have tails. Many of them are endangered.

**CAMOUFLAGE** Colors, patterns, and shapes that help an animal to blend in with its surroundings. Most night-flying moths are well camouflaged, and so are many butterflies when they close their wings. Caterpillars often use camouflage to hide themselves as they feed.

**CATERPILLAR** The larva (young form) of a butterfly or moth. Most caterpillars are cylindrical, but some are flattened or sluglike.

**CHRYSALIS** A hard outer case made by a caterpillar. The chrysalis protects the insect while it pupates, or turns into an adult butterfly or moth.

**CLASSIFICATION** A way of identifying living things, and of showing how they are linked through evolution. In classification, each type of living thing is given its own two-part scientific name. For example, the Monarch butterfly is classified as *Danaüs plexippus*, and the Painted Lady is *Cynthia cardui*. Unlike common names, scientific names can be understood all over the world.

**CLEARWING MOTHS** A group of moths that have partly transparent wings. Clearwing moths mimic stinging insects and fly by day, while their caterpillars feed on shrubs and trees.

**COCOON** A case of silk spun by many moth caterpillars when they pupate. The cocoon protects the insect while it changes into an adult—it is either attached to a plant, or buried underground.

**COURTSHIP** Special behavior used by animals when they come together to mate. In butterflies and moths, courtship often involves complex dances, as well as chemical scents that they release into the air.

**EXTINCTION** The permanent dying-out of a species of living thing. Many butterflies and moths face extinction because of deforestation and other kinds of habitat change.

**EYESPOT** An eyelike spot on the wings of a butterfly or moth. Eyespots deter predators by frightening them away.

**FAMILY** In classification, a family is a group of species that share important features. Some families of butterfly and moth contain a small number of species, but the biggest have tens of thousands.

**FOSSIL** The remains of something that died long ago, preserved in rock.

**FRITILLARY BUTTERFLIES** Butterflies with a checkered pattern on their wings. Fritillaries belong to the nymphalid family of butterflies, which have brushlike front feet.

**GANGLION** (*plural* **GANGLIA**) A cluster of nerve cells in an insect's head or in the segments of its body. Ganglia work like miniature processors, collecting information from the senses, and making muscles move.

**GENUS** (*plural* **GENERA**) In classification, a group of closely related species that have many features in common. Genera are grouped into families, and they form the first part of every species' scientific name.

**GLAND** A part of the body that makes chemical substances and releases them into the body or outside. Caterpillars make silk from special glands under the head.

**HABITAT** The surroundings in which an animal usually lives and which provide it with everything it needs to survive. Butterflies and moths live in a variety of habitats, from tropical rainforests to mountains.

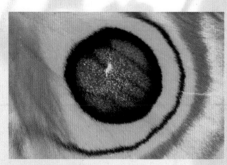

Hind-wing eyespot of Io moth

Oleander Hawkmoth,
*Daphnis nerii*

**HAIR PENCILS** Slender filaments that male butterflies and moths use to release scents into the air. They are located in the tip of the abdomen and squeezed out when in use.

**HAWKMOTHS** A group of fast-flying moths with heavy bodies and slender wings. Adult hawkmoths include many long-distance migrants, while their caterpillars include some important pests of crops.

**HIBERNATION** Spending the winter in an inactive state. Some butterflies and moths hibernate as adults, but many other species pass the winter as cold-resistant eggs.

**HORMONES** Chemical messengers that trigger changes in the way the body works. In butterflies and moths, hormones play an important part in controlling growth and molting, and metamorphosis.

**INCHWORM** *see* **LOOPER**

**INVERTEBRATE** An animal without a backbone. Invertebrates include all the world's insects, and many other animals, such as mollusks.

**LARVA** (*plural* **LARVAE**) A young animal that looks very different from its parents, and that changes shape as it matures. Caterpillars are examples of larvae—they concentrate on feeding, while adult butterflies and moths mate and lay eggs.

**LEPIDOPTERA** The order, or group, of insects that contains butterflies and moths. Lepidoptera literally means "scaly wings."

**LOOPER** The caterpillar of a geometrid moth. Loopers get their name from their unusual way of moving—their head end reaches forward, and their body then forms a loop, so that the rear "catches up."

**MANDIBLES** An insect's jaws. Unlike human jaws, mandibles form part of the exoskeleton, and they do not have teeth. They bite from side to side, instead of up and down.

**MATING** The moment when a male and female animal come together to produce young. In butterflies and moths, mating can last for several hours, and it can continue while the couple take to the air.

**METAMORPHOSIS** A change in body shape as an insect grows up. In some insects,